The Magdalene

Temple of the Divine Feminine

Mary Farrell Tobin

ISBN:1722114754
ISBN-13:9781722114756

DEDICATION

This book is dedicated to you, the Children of the Light
who have chosen to awaken and to follow your heart.

CONTENTS

Acknowledgements   i

Preface   ii

Introduction   x

Map of Israel   xvi

I.   The Early Childhood Years   1

II.   The Journey   12

III.   Qumran   20

IV.   Daughter of Isis   27

V.   Return to Qumran   54

VI.   Greece   79

VII.   Miriam of Bethany   109

VIII.   The Early Ministry   131

IX.   Child of the Light   152

Afterward   165

Glossary   170

ACKNOWLEDGMENTS

I would like to thank everyone who has supported and encouraged me to publish this book. Thank you to Andrew Talcott for creating the graphics for this book and his endless patience. I would also like to thank the people who have helped me to edit this book when my eyes became blurry from reading and re-reading the story. Thank you to my son Sean Tobin, and my friends Yvonne Dean, Jessica Farrell, Nancy Schwind, Joan Shaughnessy, and Sharon Butler O'Donnell, you are each a blessing in my life. Finally, thank you to my husband, Jack Tobin, who showed his love and faith in me by blindly following me on my great adventure to the mountains of Slovakia, the Avebury Stone Circle , and the Magdalene Almshouses in Glastonbury, where the writing of this story began.

Preface

She came to me one rainy day in the spring of 2013.

In my childhood I had come to know Mary Magdalene through the teachings of the Catholic Church and the stories of her found in the New Testament.

Later, when I was in high school, my chorus sang the song "I Don't Know How to Love Him" from the play *Jesus Christ Superstar*, and I was intrigued by Mary Magdalene's story, but beyond that she was simply a name to me, a background player in the story of Jesus.

I have always been an introspective and spiritual person and in my yearning for the mystical I began to meditate and pray the Rosary in my early 30's. During this time, I felt guided to take classes in the energy healing technique, Reiki. I became a Reiki Master in 1999 and experienced a period of tremendous transformation. In 2005, I began to open to the gifts of clairaudience and could hear clearly the voices of my spirit guides, as well as archangels and eventually the voices of the master realms. I also began to lead small groups in guided meditation. It was during this time period that I became a conduit or channel for these masters. They transmitted through me their words of wisdom and healing energy. I was, at times, overwhelmed with the information that was coming through me, but I found comfort in the discovery of several books which contained translations and interpretations of the ancient papyrus texts found near Nag Hammadi, Egypt.

Two of the books I found were *The Gnostic Gospels*, by Elaine Pagels as well as *The Gospel of Mary of Magdala,* by Karen Leigh King. Both of these books resonated deeply with me. In these books both authors share in the belief that these ancient texts were Gnostic; written by the early Christians. I felt deeply connected to the teachings and beliefs that these writings contained and this brought me a sense of peace. They also helped me to more fully

understand the messages and teachings I had
been receiving. I felt a strong resonance with
the words of Mary Magdalene in *The Gospel of
Mary of Magdala* as she spoke about the ascent
of the soul. This was a different woman than
the one who had been portrayed to me
through the church. She had a deep desire to
understand Jesus' teachings, and she herself
showed tremendous insight and wisdom. In
this Gospel Jesus shared with Mary
Magdalene many teachings, which she
continued to receive through her inner vision
after his death. She became a teacher to the
other disciples, although not all of them
accepted her in this role. I realized that I had a
deep desire to know more about this woman,
and that remained in my heart.

In the year 2012, I received a message from
my guides. They shared these words with me,
"The Notre Dame One approaches." I
continued to hear that message almost daily
for about one year, until the day when I heard
Mary Magdalene's voice. She said to me, "I
am the Notre Dame One, I am known as
Mary Magdalene, The Magdalene." I

remember feeling confused. I always believed that Notre Dame referred to The Blessed Mother. She said to me, "My name has been torn asunder. Many have tried to dismiss my teachings and my presence. I wish to speak through you so that I may be remembered once again, so that all may know my name."

We began to work together. She transmitted a six-month course through me that I called *The Magdalene Teachings*. She asked that I gather people together in groups of twelve. The groups met monthly, and she spoke and transmitted through me her teachings and healing energy. She called this course "a self-study to awaken the child of light within." It was through this work that I came to know Mary Magdalene more intimately. She told me that one day we would write together, she never explained any further than that. I've learned and accepted that when I work in this capacity as a conduit, I need to trust in the path and allow it to unfold in a synchronicity of timing.

In 2016 Mary Magdalene asked me to take on this new role, to share her story and messages through the written word. Although she has told me that I always have free will to say no to this work, Mary Magdalene can also be very persistent in reminding me that there are many people who need to hear her voice. Day and night she spoke to me of this story and the teachings she wished to share. I was uncertain of my ability to translate and write her story and questioned why I was asked to do this work. I knew that there were scholars and historians who were more knowledgeable than I was of Mary Magdalene and the ancient times of Jesus, and I also knew of other truly gifted spiritual teachers who worked with her. She repeatedly told me, " You are a witness to my being and my truth, you have a true heart."

She prepared me for what she calls "the translations" of her teachings through a series of initiations. I was guided to Slovakia, to an apparition site of The Blessed Mother; I received the blessings of Mother Mary in a small town called Litmanova. I was then guided to the henge and stone circle in Avebury, England where Kwan Yin placed her hands of light on me. My final destination was to Glastonbury, England, to a small chapel and almshouse dedicated to Mary Magdalene. Mary Magdalene, Kwan Yin, and Mother Mary joined me here for my final preparations. Gifts and wisdom that lay dormant within me were slowly awakened at these sacred sites by the light that entered me. I share this with each of you because I know that many of you are having similar experiences, experiences that you don't necessarily understand, but yet there is a inner knowing that something is happening, that you are being called. This book is part of that calling, that is why it has been placed in your hands.

This is The Magdalene's /Miriam's story, her voice spoke through my hands as I typed.

Some of the information that she shares will be new to you, as it was to me. I ask that you allow yourself to receive this story, not in an intellectual way, but through the heart. There is a tremendous amount of symbolism embedded within Mary Magdalene's story, with many layers to it, allow time for quiet reflection throughout the story.

There are many other people who have written of Mary Magdalene and her teachings; I recognize that this story is unique. If you have been drawn to these writings, then you were meant to hear this story. Allow the words to enter your heart and allow the resonance of truth within you. I felt often that we were sitting around a fire as Mary Magdalene spoke to me. She would begin a story and then add a brief memory, sometimes becoming lost in that memory before the original story was complete. I did my best to organize her memories, to honor Mary Magdalene and the story she asked me to share of her life. When I completed this writing, I found that it stirred questions within me and a deeper yearning, but I have found this to be the paradox of my spiritual journey into the mysteries.

This book is encoded with light. As you read it, you will receive these light codes into your cell structures. Allow this light activation to work in the deeper states of consciousness, to awaken the higher states of the Christ

Consciousness within you.

In the beginning you may find it difficult to follow Mary Magdalene's dialect. She says that it is not necessary that you understand her words at an intellectual level, she is speaking to the deeper aspects within you; this is where the deep knowing and understanding occurs. She wants each of you to know who she is, to remember her and her truth, and most importantly, remember your own truth as a Child of the Light.

When Mary Magdalene speaks to me, she is direct and strong. Her voice is the voice of an older woman, full of wisdom, it is deep and resonant. I feel Mary Magdalene's compassion and unconditional love when she speaks, I also feel her power. She wants each of us to step into this power and wisdom of the heart; she is waiting for you to invite her in. Her light is an indigo blue color, the light of The Blue Rose. Receive her loving presence as you read this story and come to know Mary Magdalene, or as she refers to herself, The Magdalene.

MARY FARRELL TOBIN

Introduction

I was born beneath the Star of Bethlehem. At the time of my birth, there was a star alignment that is often spoken of in regard to the Christ Structure and the Master Yeshua. Few know that on December 25th, I entered the earth as a descendent of the Book of Life, through the star system Sirius. Together we were destined to walk as one, to unite the factions of the earth.

I was born to my mother, known as Helen and my father, known by his friends and family as Benjamin. The Star of Bethlehem was a midpoint star that rose in the nighttime sky to point the way for my arrival to the great Wise Men. The Wise Men were knowledgeable in the Ways of the Mysteries. The star remained within the sky for many months.

I was named Miriam, a direct descendent of the bloodline of Benjamin. I came to aid the masses, to awaken the heart of many, and through my consecrated acts, I would bring alignment to those who seek the full Christ Structure. My companion, Yeshua, was to be born in the coming months, fulfilling the prophesies of the Book of Samuel and many others, and carrying with him the bloodline of the descendants of David.

The Magdalene Structural Template was awakened through my entrance onto the earth. It is a template of The Divine Mother energies. It enables the new bloodline to be established through the voice of The Magdalene. I am the Magdalene.
The voice of the Divine Feminine is a voice of strength and the Magdalene Structural Template holds this tower of strength and power. It brings a fiery burning away of the old structures to give voice to the new.
My work, together with the Master Yeshua, would bring the melding of the feminine and masculine, uniting two as one, to lift the veil

of forgetfulness, and the separated state.

I speak now of things not yet known to the earth, but all will become known in time. My teachings will be revealed to mankind in the coming centuries. Many ancient scriptural texts have been hidden, to be made known when the time is ripe, when the earth has been prepared and a new structure has been put in place.

I say to you now that this time is at hand. The earth and its energetic gridlines have been prepared, the crystalline structures awakened, in preparation for my teachings and the coming of the Christ Light. All heads will bow down at this coming of the dawn of The New Age. Many will be uncertain of the path, as there will be much upheaval prior to the arrival of this light and energetic surge. Those who have been well prepared will be the leaders of mankind and will guide each to the New Way. There will be a rise in fortunes. An abundant life awaits the masses, as the sacred marriage contract is awakened.

I lay bare my heart to all who would seek this truth, that they may know my ways and begin again, in the renewal of truth. That the light of heaven may once again shine forth upon this earthly dimension. This light of truth will be as a guiding force for all who would seek it. I present myself now to each of you who would hear my voice, so that the voice of The Magdalene Structure of Light, the light of the Divine Feminine may be awakened once again.

There are many would question this truth, as they know not my ways as yet. My name has been torn asunder by those who sought to diminish these teachings. Many who sought the ways of the external world have silenced the voice of the feminine. They held still the tongue of the female child, as they were fearful of the seeking of inner truths. They sought to hold sway and power over all. The thinking mind was strong within them and they drew power from the diminishment of others.

I would aid each of you in the ways of the feminine, the ways of the quiet and still mind. I would aid you that you may receive in full the cup of blessing that dwells within, that

the abundance of life may be awakened and
that each may rise to new heights and know
of their true name. Each of you who receives
my teachings will find a new voice within
them, and this voice is the voice of The
Divine, the Christ Child born again from
within your cell structures through the Divine
Union, the Sacred Marriage of old.

It is only through the silence and the ways
of the natural world that man may know all,
these are the ways of the feminine. Hear me
now, that you may awaken and remember
Dear Ones, as these truths dwell within you.
We shall begin again, and all shall come to
know my name, The Magdalene One. It is a
title I have held in centuries past, I claim it
once again, that the tower, the inferno
structure, may be laid bare for all to see, that
the divine countenance may be awakened in
full within all who seek it.

I would speak to you now of my birth and
early childhood years, so that I may awaken
the memory center within each of you, as each
who hears my words at present has walked
with me and knows the truths that I speak.

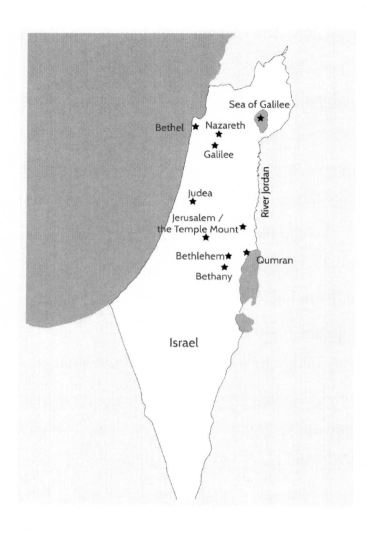

I

The Early Childhood Years

I have often thought of my early childhood years as a time of fond memories, as there was much play and laughter in them. My father was of a tall stature, broad shouldered and strongly guided by the spirit of The Most High. He was swift to anger, though slow to judge those in need. He was given the name of Cyrus, though he was known in our tribe as Benjamin. Cyrus was from the royal bloodline of the tribe of Benjamin. He was of a priestly nature, and he carried with him a majestic line that allowed him, the eldest son, to be a man of great wealth and properties.

He held a high standing in the community of Bethel, the place of my birth, and often spoke at the gatherings of the High Priests at the Rabbinical Center. He was of a strong debate manner, arguing often against any injustices witnessed by him. Benjamin was a father to many and spoke in kind tones to the youth of my village, often laughing and engaging in their play. He was inclined to aid those in need and spent his days in small group gatherings, speaking often of the needs of the community and bringing those needs before the High Council. Benjamin was of a strong countenance as well. None would seek to speak against him, for he was swift to respond, and was of a highly educated mind.

Often, we would walk together, and he would speak to me of the High Heavens and share with me the vastness of his knowledge. He was knowledgeable of the ways of the Ancients, and the Great Mysteries as well. He knew of the Ascent of Man and sought to aid me in understanding of these matters, though he spoke often in allegory, as I was but a child.

We walked often in the nearby forests, and he spoke to me of the trees and the ways of nature, helping my child's mind to open to the vastness of life and the truths that lie hidden in the rustling of the leaves and the winds that blow. I often held his hand as we walked, and he spoke in a gentle way to me, as he knew of the strong influence he had upon my impressionable mind. He knew as well of my great destiny; that it was important that I be strongly guided upon the path of The Way. He spoke to me often of the nature of reality, and the truths that lied hidden there. And, as I was of a child's mind, I saw clearly these truths.

I spoke to the Elohim and to the Angelic Realm that accompanied us on these walks. I saw clearly their flickering lights and felt the brush of their wingtips upon my cheek. My father sought to expand my vision in regard to the Higher Realms, to those who were of a guiding nature to me. He listened thoughtfully to his own inner visions and guidance and spoke to me of these guiding forces. His knowledge of the Ancients was vast, as the teachings had been handed down to him through his paternal bloodline, and he had clear sight to these truths. I placed great trust in my father; he showed patience with my intrepid nature and questioning of all things that were not of this world. He embraced me often and laughed loudly when I wiggled away to explore some new adventure, as the forest called to me as did no other.

Often, we would gaze at the stars at night and I saw about me the strings of light that floated freely both around me and within me. We would lie side by side in the fields near our home, and he would point to the Belt of Orion, naming each star. My father would guide me in the understanding of each star's placement in the heavens and its significance to mankind. He helped me to understand that the movement of the stars and planets created energetic shifts within me, which, when I was fully aligned, allowed me to advance in my earthly studies. He explained that it was through the advancement of the equinox settings and our alignment with the stars, that mankind advanced as well, as each of us was fully connected, both within and without, to these systems. It is only those with a negligent heart who would disconnect from this alignment and thus create a stagnant and avoidant stature.

As a child I felt the vibratory pull of these settings within me and through the magnetic pull of the earth's grid beneath my feet. I would gaze steadily at the stars and feel their flames within me, and as I walked the earth I felt the star's gaze upon me as they aligned with the earth's grid.

My mother was of an ancient lineage. Her birth name was Miriam as well, as she was of the ancient order of The Magdalene Structure, and claimed her birth name as one of this ancient order of High Priestesses. She was of a great and nurturing nature. She held me tight to her breastbone often. Lovingly she held me, and often wiped the tears from my eyes when one of my great adventures ended in a fall or injury. She was slow to anger, and of a compassionate heart. She yielded to many and my father would often reprimand her for being too giving to others who would take advantage of her kind nature. Although her given name was Miriam, those close to her knew her as Helen. She was a direct descendent of the Maccabee blood-line.

As the eldest child, my mother spoke to me often as a small confidant. She would speak to me of others in our village and often point out ridicule or gossip, guiding me to speak kindly of others. I dearly loved my mother; I would often entwine my hands within her long locks of hair, seeking closeness with her warmth. She made the salted bread daily, as she knew it to be my favorite.

Though my father was of a great and intellectual capacity, my mother had insight and knowledge as well. She was well bred in the teachings of the path of The Way and was considered to be a woman of great healing gifts. Many would turn to her when a fever or illness would overtake them. She had knowledge of herbal remedies and carried with her chamomile, hyssop, feverfew, the dandelion herb, and many others. She emanated from her being a gentle and loving grace; it softly touched all that surrounded her.

All spoke with tremendous reverence of my mother. She knew of the ways of the Ancients, and would often place her hands upon those who were ill, drawing from them the darkness that blocked the movement of light within the energetic vein structures. She learned of these techniques from my grandmother, of my maternal bloodline. My grandmother knew of the healing touch and many other techniques of healing. She would often include the use of stones upon the body, seeking the energetic vibrations akin to the gemstone. They would be placed upon the heart, or some such area that had lost its innate rhythms, in the hopes of regaining the gentle flow of energetic light.

My mother was a great teacher as well, as she was of the lineage of the High Priestesses of Isis. She gathered many to her and led them onto the Path of Light. She followed a strict code of ethics, known only to those who were knowledgeable of these teachings. I learned much from my mother and grandmother of the Ways of Light. These techniques were passed from mother to child over many generations, though all knew that the original teachings came from foreign lands far across the sea.

The lands of which I speak had long ago sunk beneath the ocean waves. To some, this place was known as Atlantis. Atlantis resided in an ancient time period in the history of man in which the great masters walked among us. There were many there who studied the stars in the sky and had great knowledge of the Universe. Atlantis resided not on one continent per se, but on many shifting land patterns that have been lost to the sea. Advanced technologies were created there through the scientific studies of the earth's grid lines and systems. There was knowledge of the use of stones that allowed for great healing of the physical form.

The study and knowledge of crystals has been well documented in other writings of Atlantis. I would say to each of you that there are great truths in these writings, and I would add to this information that there were many great wisdom keepers who resided in this place, who embedded within the crystalline grid system the knowledge that they held. These keepers of knowledge have been born once again and walk amongst you now, Dear Ones. They hold the keys to these interlocking pavers that reside beneath your feet. It is through the activation process of the memory centers within them that the keys to these grid systems may be awakened. It is to this work that I have been called. To awaken the hearts of those of you who hold these keys of wisdom. I beckon my hand to you to join with me. To awaken the keys within you, that the knowledge of the Ancients may be once again brought forth to aid the Earth. The grid system that dwells in the inner earth has been brought on line in these times, Little Ones. I guide you to dwell within and to remember. Allow your memory centers to awaken so that the keys within you may unlock these crystalline grids and release the vast storage centers of wisdom. I guide you to remember, that the knowledge of the Ancients may dwell once again upon the Earth. That you may walk again as masters, holding new structures of light that allows the Universe and your brethren in the star systems beyond to expand exponentially through the anchoring in of your starlight. The Atlantean times dwell within each of you, remember and draw them forth.

Atlantis was an advanced society of great abundance. Many there were of an enlightened state within the vast number of societies contained within it. They held a high vibrational frequency that allowed the great Manifestor God to be awakened within them.

Some of the knowledge of these masters was passed down and came to us through a travelling band who entered the land of Egypt and travelled forth to aid the masses, less the knowledge that they held be lost. The healing stones acquired by my mother and her sisters were passed from these people, known to us as the Galactic Ones, the Annanaki. They were an indigenous tribe, descended from these ancient lands. The travelling ones were spoken of often within the inner circles of my people. The knowledge they brought to us was a secret knowledge to be shared only with those of a pure heart who would use it wisely.

My father was considered a great leader of my tribe. He carried the knowledge of the Annanaki teachings, though he spoke to few of this knowledge outside of our inner circles. His brothers knew of these ways of old and sought out the leadership of my father. They trusted in his guidance to lead our tribe.

II

The Journey

It was at the ripe age of three that I departed with my family from the place of my birth. My father was guided to begin this journey in preparation for the days of the prophecies that were to come. Though few knew of my father's true knowledge, they trusted that he was divinely guided to begin this journey. The Most High assigned him this role, to lead us forth from the village of Bethel to the place called Qumran. Qumran was known to us to be a community center where we would dwell to aid in the anchoring in process of the Great Teachings, and to prepare for the coming of The Righteous One.

We created settlements in the nearby lands of Bethel. We would remain for months at a time in these settlements before departing to create the next one. During this time, we allowed energetic shifts to occur within each of us, in preparation for our movement forward to the land of Qumran. We slept often beneath the open sky, though sometimes a small tent would be prepared, three sided, allowing ventilation yet protection from the elements. We would rise early, my mother gently shaking me and telling me to prepare for the day's journey. We would travel prior to the rising of the Sun, allowing us to travel before the intense gaze of the Sun, which often beat down upon our backs and forced us to begin our rest in the early afternoon.

We lived together in companionship with many who sought out a new life. My father embraced them each. During this period of time I enjoyed much comradeship with the other children, and great prestige as well as the daughter of Benjamin. I often felt compelled to remain by my father's side.

There were many hardships during these days. The men often travelled far to obtain food and necessities, but we enjoyed the freedom of this life. I embraced it fully and learned from those who were around me. We sought the true nature of things through the study of what was about us.

There were many who accompanied us on this journey; some were family members from my paternal family structure. My father was one of seven brothers. Three accompanied us on our journey along with their wives and children, my beloved cousins, with whom I often played and explored the countryside. There was one cousin who brought me great joy in my early years, my cousin Gabriel. He was of a joyful nature and fearless in his ways. Together we sought many adventures, much to our parents' chagrin. We were apt to wander off, seeking new adventures amongst the rock formations nearby. My cousin Abraham was often sent to find us. He would reprimand us sternly, though he would give us a gentle smile when the lecture was complete. He had a true understanding of our need for adventure and play and would engage us in small story telling about the fire at night. I had great affection for Abraham, the son of my father's brother Zebediah. He was as a fatherly nature to me and spoke to me often of the Ways of Light and the twinkling stars above. He had an intellectual mind and would often spend time during the day with me as we travelled, speaking of his great insights and the mathematical equations corresponding to the nighttime sky and the Great Equinox of the Sun. I was in awe of his intellect, and listened with rapt attention as he spoke. I did not understand his words, though the concepts of which he spoke entered me and remained with me in my later years. His gentle words had great resonance in my cell structures.

The walking regiment was an important
part of our daily practice. It was often in the
evening that we would take gentle walks,
sometimes in small groups, and at other times
in a singular fashion. I enjoyed these times,
walking often with my father upon the desert
land, accompanied by my cousins. My mother
and aunts would prepare the meals and take
their walks later, after the preparation of the
food. We walked along the upper banks of the
nearby rivers, though often our travels took us
to small forest structures as well. We would
laugh together, holding hands, speaking of the
day, anticipating the new land of Qumran and
the hope that we placed there. My father
would speak to us of this place, sharing with
us its holy nature. He sought to aid us in our
understanding that this place would bring
salvation to many, as it held within it the true
teachings of our bloodline. Each of us would
hold a space within it and would be called to
play a role in preserving these teachings. In
our child's minds we fantasized our roles and
saw ourselves as the great adventurers. As we
walked, my father would speak of the

gemstones that were held safe within the walls of this Qumran place. He would describe their beauty and promise that each of us would have an opportunity to hold the sparkling stones. He spoke of the great power that they contained and would ask each of us to extend our hands as he placed small, minute pieces of the stones in the palm of our hands. I would feel the weight of these gemstones, though in truth they were no more than pebbles, and feel the palm of my hand increase in size as the stone rested there. There would be a great and magnetic pressure that built within me as I held the stone, and my chest cavity felt as if it would burst through the power of this small pebble. These stones were of varying sizes and lengths and would glisten in the sunlight. I knew them to be rose quartz, hematite, and a small green stone known as malachite. There were many others that were introduced to us as well. I held tight to one in particular and placed it close to my heart as it had great resonance within me. It was known as blue lapis. In future years this stone would become known to me more fully as a great protector of the light within me, and I would keep it with me often.

A campfire would be set in the evening at the completion of our repast, and together we would sit, engaging in storytelling and sharing of the day. The children would listen in rapt attention, eagerly hoping for an opportunity to engage as well, though we dared not unless asked directly to share or speak. We knew and understood that this was the time for our elders to rest, to laugh together and to make plans for the coming day. There would be a nod of the head from my father or one of the elders when it was time for us to rest, and my cousin Natalie would whisk us away, as she was the eldest female cousin and was of a mothering nature.

When the time came for us to travel to Qumran, we walked daily for many days. We were hastened by the Sun's daily glare and the nighttime visions that my father shared with the tribe, of the coming of the Messiah and our need to be present to aid in his Great Work. My father knew of the Messiah's coming through the teachings and his studies of the rabbinical texts. He was also guided by the inner visions that spoke to him of the coming days. My Father knew that we were well protected by the Angelic Realm in the Great Work and so he entrusted our care to the Heavenly Hosts that were about us.

We arrived in Qumran on the third day of the third month, a number sequence that was significant for the journey of the heart and the days that lay before us.

III

Qumran

I was of a child's nature in those early years of my life, impetuous and quick to jump without thought. My father would shake his head and laugh gently at my exploits. My mother would hold me tight, sternly reprimanding me, though I often saw the teasing nature in her eyes. They understood my ways, and in truth were of an encouraging nature. Quick to laugh, and joyous in my ways, I brought a smile to the lips of many.

My father and mother knew of my true nature and encouraged me to allow my vessel of pure light to shine. They did not over wrestle with a need to dominate or subjugate my inner instincts, but were firm in their disciplining of my sometimes over -zealous nature. The use of firm boundaries is necessary for a child of early years so that they may know that they are well cared for and loved.

My father knew, as did my mother, that my birth had been prognosticated and would fulfill many prophecies. They knew that in fulfillment of these prophesies, I would speak to the masses, and help to guide them on the Path of Light. I knew of this in my child's heart and would often hear the song of my heart reverberating through my cell structures. The song was of a joyous nature, and I would wonder that others did not hear it, as it was plain to me and harmonized with the songs that were about me. I heard the music of the trees and the birds, and I would feel these harmonies enter me, entwining within my heart and giving birth to new life within me through the twists and turns of the light body. As the song within my heart harmonized with the Earth's rhythms, I would feel a connection, strong and powerful. The Earth Mother would speak to me of her great love, which would pulsate throughout my being, and it would seem that I might burst with the joy that I found at these times.

My mother understood and spoke often of these harmonies of the Earth and the world that was about us. She would speak of the joy, and guide me gently to rest in the quiet, to allow time to hear the Earth Mother, to lay upon her and know of this deep connection.

The energies that moved through me when I connected with the Earth would spiral within me, and in the nighttime hours this dance would bring me to the outer limits of the sky above. Often, I would travel, floating gently upon the ocean breezes and then upward to the mountaintops, where many would gather with me. I knew my teachers from the other realms. They would speak to me of my great purpose and guide me in the ways of the world, as well as the outer expanses of the Universe. My Earth's mission was strong within me, and I embraced it in full. I knew I had been placed within my family to be cared for and nurtured by the outer teachings of the Judaic system and lineage. I knew as well that the day would come when I would be called to a higher duty and that I would work with others who would prepare me for the destiny that was at hand.

The teachers that I speak of would approach in my early teenage years, and it would be through them that I would receive the inner teachings, as an Initiate of the Daughters of Isis. My mother would speak of these women often, quietly whispering in my ear as I drifted to sleep, knowing that I travelled to them in the nighttime hours.

A richness of devotional prayer life was a central theme in my upbringing in Qumran. The chanting rhythms of the Aramaic language began and ended our day, as did the teachings of the Torah, often read by my father as we broke bread together prior to the evening walks. The Rabbinical studies of which I speak, enabled my mind to expand as I explored these outer teachings, as much was symbolic and of an allegorical nature.

My duties were few as a young child. I was required to aid my mother in the drawing of water from the nearby river. I was also called to aid in the preparation of food, often consisting of risen bread, vegetables, and sometimes grains accompanied by a fruit. There were many herbs used in the preparation of food, as gardening was a joyous pastime for many in Qumran, often yielding great quantities of food due to our dedication, the great amount of sun, and our knowledge of the Earth's magnetics. Our gardens were well placed, in synchrony with the Earth's grid. Often stones were placed about the grid lines to aid in the growth of plants, this created energetic surges of light that entered the plant from the Earth's gridlines. We knew the fault-lines of the Earth as well, and we were careful to farm far away from areas that were known to be of a shifting nature. The heart-lines of the earth were important to the growing of crops, and when the plants were well placed upon these lines of energy the plants thrived and grew, often exponentially. I enjoyed helping my mother in the gardens, as it was play to me. I would speak often to the plants and flowers and they would respond to me in a whistling song, which I understood to be their true voice. It harmonized well with my energies and allowed me to feel them more fully.

The heart and its reverberations are a key component to the Earth's mission of each Being of Light that enters this dimensional body. It is through listening to the heart and aligning it well to the Earth's rhythms and grid lines that much changeover is allowed to take place within the light-body.

The harmonies of the Earth are akin to a masterful symphony, and it is through the child-like nature within each of us that this symphony can be heard.

IV

Daughter of Isis

Bend now your ear to me, as I will speak to you of the great teachings that were imparted to me in the years prior to my life's mission with my companion Yeshua. Let the mask now be lifted that all may now hear my voice and know of the great truths that I speak.

I will speak of my days of learning. I was an inquisitive child, sure of my thoughts, though my curiosity knew no bounds. My father showed great patience with me and would often take me aside during the book learning periods of the day, to allow my questions to be fully answered and my inquisitive mind satiated. There were vast libraries in the Qumran settlement, brought by many who walked the earth and collected vessels of knowledge, placing them within the archives of the library. The ones of whom I speak were close to my father, as he was a curator to these vast vessels of knowledge, and sought to protect them from those who were not of our ways and had not the understanding to embrace these truths.

My father and I would sit side-by-side, and together we would explore the Books of the Ancients. Their knowledge was vast, and it brought me great peace to learn of their ways and knowledge of the Universe, because in truth these thoughts often entered my mind as well, though I knew not from whence they had come to me.

I had a deep connection with the philosophical teachings of Pythagoras, though the knowledge of numbers and equations was often beyond the span of my mind. I embraced the writings of the great philosophers, however, it was the teachings of the Ancients from the land known as Atlantis that I most resonated, as their knowledge of the workings of crystals and the energies of the Earth was akin to my own.

These ancient texts, as I have told you, were carried to us by the vessels of this great lineage. They carried these books of knowledge across a vast expanse of land and sought out the tribes who would honor the teachings, that they not be lost, but forever carried, both through voice and through pen to ink. It was to my father that they would visit, though it was often in the nighttime hours when others would sleep. When my father spoke to me of these entities of light, he spoke with great reverence. He would share their teachings with me and with those who sought the Inner Light.

These teachings were in stark contrast to many of the rabbinical teachings, which were often of a puritanical nature. The teachings of the Rabbis' sought to cleanse the outer being, whereas the teachings of the Ancients brought to light the cleansing of the inner vehicle, which allowed each of us to rise to new heights in the expansion of the heart and mind. It was this truth that brought forth much happiness within me, as this was the knowledge that I sought as I explored the library of Qumran and repeatedly knocked on the door of the heavenly realms.

My father sought to shield me from the world around us, offering protection from the diminishing tongues and the gossiping nature of some, both within our village and in the surrounding areas. I was privileged, educated in a unique way from other children. The females of my community were allowed access to these teachings, though we were few in number in contrast to the male gender.

My sister Martha had little interest in these teachings and sought a life closer to home. I was the eldest child, and as such, Martha deferred to me often, allowing me to be the leader of the group, as did my brother Lazarus. Lazarus was the youngest, and my father found great joy in him. He held my sister in high affection as well, though he was gentle with her as she was of a sensitive nature. The communal living, which my family enjoyed, allowed each of us much freedom in our choices, a privilege not given to those in the nearby cities and villages. The children of these areas had a strict upbringing, and followed guidelines established by the Sanhedrin, the High Priests of the area. These children suffered sharp rebuke in response to questions of their religious upbringing. I was of a unique nature in that my parents chose to separate from their tribe of origins and enter the Qumran community. My father was one of high standing both within the community of Qumran and of Bethel. His influence was great upon many, and there were none who questioned him upon his departure from the city of Bethel.

My father sought to aid me in my

advancement of knowledge and would bring
me often to the land of Egypt. The land of
Alexandria was a place of exploration, as were
the Egyptian Temples. As my father was
known to be a traveler, his travels to foreign
cities was accepted by the Qumran
community. My mother would sometimes join
us on these journeys, accompanied by my
brother and sister. It was during one visit in
particular that my footsteps would take a turn
onto a new path of learning.

My father led us on a journey to the
Egyptian cities to visit the great temples. As
my mother had accompanied us on this
journey we sought out the priestesses of the
Temple of Luxor. This was a place my mother
knew well from her own early learning years.
The priestesses there were kind and
remembered her, as she bore the Veil of
Light, it could be seen clearly by their inner
vision. Upon my presentation to these ones, a
great and glorious light entered into the tomb

structure of the underground tunnels in which we dwelled. This light permeated the temple structure, and all that resided there could feel this strong vibration. The light-body of each present there expanded, and a great and resounding "Yes" was heard throughout. I heard and felt this "Yes" enter me. It expanded my heart and I felt compelled to lay prostrate upon the floor of the tunnel structure. Upon my rising, my mother and all who dwelled within this structure, placed their hands gently upon my forehead, for they knew of this great and glorious call and sought to place a sign of benediction upon me. I received it well.

So, it was at the age of thirteen I entered the Temple of Luxor, within the inner chambers, and began my journey as a Daughter of Isis. I received the inner teachings and the ancient initiations into the Light Body of the Divine Feminine, that I might be fully prepared as an Annunciate of the Chalice of Divine Functioning. My father rejoiced in this, though my mother was tearful and embraced me, reluctant to leave me.

It was on the third day, following this initiatic rite, that my parents departed from Egypt, and my new assignment as a Priestess Apostolate began. I rejoiced in this new assignment and embraced in full this new life that the Great Goddess had brought to me in my hour of need.

The Goddess Isis was an embodiment of the Divine Mother, the Great Goddess. I knew her to be of a great and loving nature, strong in her ways of wisdom. She spoke to us through the inner vision of the High Priestess, though I often heard her voice in the nighttime hours, and was guided by her in my daily practices. My father had well-formed my inner vision as a young child, so the practice of meditation and quiet was well versed to me.

There were other young apostolates that joined me in my daily duties, and I bonded strongly with them on this new adventure. It was upon our early rising that we invoked the voice of the Great Goddess to speak to us, that we might be instruments to be used in full, so that the grace of her being may be awakened upon our earthly form.

Daily we practiced and listened to her inner teachings, and upon completion we shared the voice within us and contemplated this voice of wisdom with the elders of the priestess temple. They would speak often to us of their own inner wisdom, guiding us upon the Path of Light, and seeking to awaken us to the Inner Mysteries of Life.

The High Priestess would take us often into nature, where we would learn of the natural flow of the rivers that bound the land. She would liken these rivers to the flow of the sustenance of light within our blood, its slow movement drawing forth great change within our systems as the light nourished our being. We were taught that it was through the natural flow of light within, that all nature entered into a divine state. Just as the river flows through the land and brings nourishment and cleansing to the physical form and all who seek it, so too did this flow of light within our bloodstream bring nourishment and cleansing to our Body of Light.

We cleansed often in the waters, as the waters were of a strong mineral base and drew forth the toxins from within our systems, allowing the light force energy to flow more freely. We laughed and played within these waters, the River Nile as it was known, as we were yet still young girls. Our laughter brought forth smiles to the elders of our tribe as well. When all was complete, and our physical forms cleansed, we moved forward to the day, moving once again into the inner temples, through doorways and passages where others dare not tread. Many would see us enter, and they knew of our great lineage, but it created great fear within them and they would look away, uncertain of our ways, and the places that we entered.

There were many staircases within the inner temples; they traveled below the Temple of Luxor, to the inner earth as it were, close to the heart rhythms of the Earth Mother. She spoke to us often through her gentle rhythms and pulsations of light. The Earth Mother spoke to us of the great darkness that grew within her as well. Many who did not seek the

Ways of the Heart had implanted this darkness within the earth. They sought to reject the earth and her mothering ways. They dug deep into her cave structures and excavated and mined her for the great riches of the Earth. The seeds of darkness had become implanted within these mines and grew strong and steady, as there were few to aid in the clearing of the darkness that grew. She spoke often to us of this darkness, and implored us to help her, as she too sought to rise in full to the Great Light of Divine Function, but was held bound by this darkness. We heard her voice well, and vowed to aid her, to move into her great caverns and molten rocks, to excavate in full this darkness that lay heavy upon the Earth.

We knew of the Dark Ones, though we did not speak of them often, preferring to focus our mind's eye upon the Great Light. Our forefathers, the ancients of old, passed this knowledge down to us. It was through these teachings that we knew of the dark seeds that had been planted within the womb of many, giving birth to a race of man, no longer fully emblazoned with the Seed of Light, degraded to a lesser form. These Dark Ones sought to diminish and enslave. They sought the insatiable hunger of power through the neglect of the heart. These Dark Ones remain to this day, Little Ones. You know them well, through their need to feed on the diminishment of others. The planting of their dark seeds has diminished the capacity of many to rise to their true light. The Dark Ones feed on this diminishment through hooking into the power source of others, the Hard-Core Center. They seek to deter each from the Path of Light through their abuse of power structures and this hooking in process. The less-than status has known its beginnings through the work of these dark sorcerers.

I speak to you now of this, Little Ones, so that you may come to know once again of your true source of light within. That you may gain access once again to your truth and to the power source of the Hard-Core Center, the diamond structure, and I say to you now that it is through the true and loving heart that all access is gained.

My father spoke of these ones to me. He
taught me of their rise to power upon the
Earth. It was through this rise that the fall of
Atlantis, a great nation of mankind, occurred.
There were many who tried to protect the
Earth at that time, and it is through them that
much wisdom was carried to safety and
hidden when the great wave covered the
Earth and brought devastation to all who
dwelled there.

These teachings remain hidden, hidden
now Little Ones, to be discovered when
mankind is ready to once again hold these
great teachings to their hearts. When the
seeking of external powers no longer holds
mankind spellbound, and the ways of the
heart are once again returned and anchored
into the Earth.

I return you now to the Inner Temples of
Luxor, where I and many other Initiates
dwelled, in full joy in the living. It was here

that we lived and rejoiced in the teachings of the Great Mystery School of Isis.

The Divine Mother was known to us as the Egyptian Goddess Isis, as this was the ancient lineage each of us had chosen prior to our incarnation. There were other schools as well, such as those of the Great Goddess Aphrodite and the Celtic Goddess Brighid. One such school to which we were closely associated was the lineage of The Order of Mechilzedek. Their teachings were vast and were open only to those who were of a pure heart and listened within the heart to these teachings. My father and mother were each of the chosen bloodlines of Melchizedek. They had entered the inner temples and knew of these teachings. My parents had been well prepared for my upbringing.

The Temple of Luxor was of a glorious nature during the time in which I dwelled. It vibrated with an inner light, and this light entered into all that dwelled within it. My heart would sometimes pound during the nighttime hours as the light entered, waking me. Eventually my heart quieted as the angels gently placed their wings about me.

I studied the stars with my brethren, my Sisters in the Light. We would begin in the early evening tide and await the arrival of the first star to shine in the night-time sky. Upon its arrival, we each would clap our hands, knowing that our adventure was about to begin. The star system Sirius was the system we most often studied, as it brought to us great knowledge, and awakened our hearts to the truth of our light. Its light reverberated throughout our system upon its arrival, and we felt a kinship to it, knowing that it was from this place that each of us had come, prior to our arrival upon the Earth. We knew of our truth as Star Seeds.

The High Priestess taught us of the life within and of the ascending and descending movement of currents that entered and exited the physical form and cycled back again into the energetic structure. We learned of these movements, of the undulating light, the coil that lay often asleep at the base of the spine. Together we learned to awaken this energy, and to draw its gentle movement up the spinal column. These energies would enter the heart and draw forth new rhythms within it, emboldening and strengthening the heart as it awakened to a new light, and as this burst of light occurred, it would enter the forehead structure as well. The cycle completed when it entered the sacral area once again. It was through the awakening of the heart's energies that the light would flow seamlessly through the energetic system, awakening the mind's eye and drawing forth a great quaking and shaking within. It was upon the completion of this energy cycle that a new life would be born within. All was made new. And as we became knowledgeable of this light-cycle, we would practice it daily.

We renewed our vows, and began anew, to heightened states of awareness, to a new state of peace within. We began to know of a uniformed form, the pulsating waveforms of light entered and moved fluidly throughout our systems. It often drew forth bouts of laughter for the great joy that entered.

As I entered my High Initiate status, the Peace of the Dove entered me, and a sweet, perfumed state began to emanate from my being. It was of a frankincense nature and sought to awaken the true heart. I wore a single ruby ring; I bore it on my left hand. It was both of a symbolic nature and curative as well. The ruby ring symbolized the new title that had entered me, and the high stature and queenly state of my being, the new prowess that I had attained. It symbolized as well the red light that had entered into my sacral area, anchoring me down inward to a surrendered state, so that I may be a true vessel of light, to serve in full the light that surrounded and pervaded my being. The ruby stone contained great curative powers as well. Its light entered my bloodstream, clearing old energy passageways and growing strong my heart and its rhythms.

I dwelled for many years in the Temple of Luxor, in an idyllic place of joy, warm in the embrace of the priestesses and the apostolates that had entered with me.

It was in my seventeenth year that my life's mission became more firmly implanted within me. My father came often to visit me in the Egyptian land, my mother less often, though she sent messages of love and many gifts of herbal remedies and such. It was upon my father's visit in my seventeenth year that he transferred to me the knowledge that there approached a time of the fulfillment of the scriptural texts. He spoke of the young Yeshua, who was now in apprenticeship to my kinsman, Joseph. My father had deep knowledge of the great works that Yeshua would bring, he knew of Yeshua's studies and the depth of his wisdom, as Yeshua studied often with my father at Qumran; he was a seeker of the wisdom of the great mysteries. My father spoke to me of Yeshua with reverence, though he remained a youth as yet. He sought to aid me in my understanding so that I might come to know and accept my role in the coming years.

I listened with rapt attention to the stories my father told me. Yeshua performed great feats, even at his young age, and baffled the minds of the masters in his knowledge of the stars and the intricate settings of the Equinox cycles. My father spoke with great warmth of Yeshua's true and loving nature, and his natural inclination to lead others; to be in his presence was to be in a strong and powerful presence of light. All who were near to him felt this great light and were drawn to it. This, my father said, was the sign of a true prophet, a master among men, who would lead the masses, and draw forth great change within them.

Yeshua had shown great interest in me and the Teachings of Isis during his time with my father. He was well versed in the teachings of the matriarchal lineage as his mother was of a learned stature and had also followed the path as a Priestess of Isis.

There were many within our communities who were knowledgeable of the matriarchal lineage, as in truth it was this lineage that extended to the beginning times. It was through the matriarchal lineage that the process of creation had extended to the Earth. It was the Divine Creatrix that enlivened the Earth and gave birth to new life within it. All truth seekers knew of these teachings, and revered the mother energies and the primal cause of life and conception. It was this Divine Lineage that had inspired me to follow the path of light to the mother image of Isis, as she was an embodiment of this truth from ancient times, and could be found throughout the Earth, bearing the face of many names. It was through the powers of deception that the patriarchal bloodline became the dominating force upon the Earth, through the seeking of external forces and power structures. The use of this force upon the Earth brought low to the ground the capacity of the Earth to enliven and to be reborn. The Earth, over the thousands of years that had preceded my entrance, became a place of dominion over, though it once was a place of true peace and equanimity.

The land of Nod was such a place, where the matriarchy and patriarchy dwelled together as one, the strong Creatrix well protected and emboldened by the paternal bloodline. It is spoken of in mythic terms, though in truth, it was a place of greatness, where the true capacity of life lived and dwelled.

Over eons past, the dominating masculine energies have brought an imbalance within the energetic form of mankind. These energies can only be brought back into balance through the ways of the heart and the Divine Feminine. The ways of the Ancient Mysteries have called this the sacred marriage, the heirgamos.

The Goddess Aphrodite and many others came as embodiments of the Divine Feminine. The Goddess Artemis carried the

Light of Divine Wisdom and the Power of
Prophesy. The Celtic Goddess Brighid was a
strong warrior goddess, and held within her
the Celtic Weave of Life. They all carried
within them the many and varied aspects of
the Divine Feminine. At the time of my
father's meeting with me, I knew myself to be
an embodiment of this ancient wisdom line.
There had been implanted within my being,
structures of this wisdom, and from it a
wellspring of knowledge would be drawn
forth.

I would speak now of my direct lineage to
the Sheba One, known to you as The Queen
of Sheba. She was of an ancient lineage which
carried within it great power. She was noble
and stood strong and tall in this power. The
Sheba One was of an Ethiopian origin and
knew of her great value and worth. The
lineage of which I now speak was from the
line of Benjamin, my father's lineage. The
Sheba One had sprung forth from this ancient
lineage and she too was born as the
embodiment of the mother image. Her seeds
had been planted in my bloodline and this

bloodline sought to continue to the children of my children so that new cycles of life could spring forth from it. I carried with me the seeds of this lineage, implanted within me prior to my light conception.

I hold now within my hand the Seeds of Light that are yet to be implanted within you. They hold the Light of the Feminine. I would see them implanted within each of you who read these words that you may awaken to your truth.

My father knew of this truth, and fully acknowledged me as this embodiment. He knew of the role that he was called to play in the awakening of these prophesies within me.

It was through my father's bloodline that a new and yet ancient lineage would begin anew.

A new bloodline that would dance in the rhythms of the Earth and establish a new order upon this earthly plain.

A divine heritage that would awaken the heart of

mankind so that each may dance once again in the light-body of old.

I came to anchor in the Goddess aspects of love and wisdom. The counterpart to my being was to be the Christ structure embodied by the Master Yeshua. Together we were to form a divine union, to awaken the heart of many, that the Christ Child, the Child of the Divine within each may be brought forth.

My father spoke to me of these things to me and we laughed and cried in a joyous nature. We knew of the days to come. My father recited prayers of benediction upon me prior to his departure so that a new cycle may be awakened within me. My time of preparation would begin.

My mother passed gently into a new life's passage during my eighteenth year. A message was sent to me of her passage, and I wept openly for her gentle nature and my longing for the tender years of my youth. We began a new relationship over time and she became a guide to me. I felt her more strongly in my later years, but she remained by my side throughout.

My father, I learned in my nineteenth year, was of a diminished capacity, no longer able to wander freely to visit me, and to speak of his vast knowledge of things.

My education was complete at the age of twenty-one years. I had attained an acclaimed status as a High Initiate in the Priestess Teachings of Isis. As a High Initiate, I was held in high regard by many, and my teachings were sought after by the newly initiated, and by the people who travelled through the land of Egypt, in search of the educated and those who would aid them on their path to enlightenment. Though those numbers were few, my days were kept busy by the many teachings that passed through my lips and by my time in quiet revelry with the Divine.

I would often be found taking quiet walks along the riverbed. I sought out stones of high vibration during these journeys and would place them within my small pouch made of leather. I would hold these stones close to my breastbone as the pouch hung around my neck, tucked well beneath the inner clothes that bound me. I felt their resonance within me and felt as well a kinship with their energetic form, as they helped me in releasing old energy forms that no longer served my current form. They were drawn to me from the Earth Mother, who placed them upon my path, and I would feel a gentle tingling sensation as I approached the stones.

I saw clearly now through my interior vision, my path as a Divine Mission of Love, well laid and planned from above. I had incarnated in this time period to aid the Master Yeshua, and as the time drew near for our meeting, I could sense the increasing light and vibration within me. It was magnetic at times, a lodestone, drawing me near to him, though he as yet lived in a distant land.

My father had administered to me well, so I knew of the prophecies that preceded Yeshua. The prophet Isaiah had spoken of his return to aid the masses, to draw forth the resurrected form. Yeshua was of a True and Divine Lineage of Light, his forebears, from the ancient line of David, had prepared this line. It is from the Book of Life that I now speak. The Enochian and his ancient Language of Light had also spoken of the return of light to the Earth and of the embodied spirit of light that would carry it. It spoke of the return of the Christed one, who would hold the light for many.

The Messengers of Light, of the Angelic Realm, invoked his name to aid us in our hour of need, so that the Temple of Divine Structure would dwell once again upon this Earth. It was through this ancient lineage that a light would shine forth and bring a New Earth, of a divine function, co-created in the name of love, and all would ascend to new heights.

V

Return to Qumran

In my 21st year, I returned home. Though my mother was no longer there, my father remained in the village of Qumran, and it was here that I found him, one early morning tide. He rested gently among the flowers of the fields; he sensed my presence and gently opened his eyes in warm greeting. As my father had always been strong and of a tall stature, it was a shock to my system to see that in my time away from him, he had become frail, withered in his hands and

hunched to his side as he rose to greet me.
There was a weakness to his grip as he
embraced me, though his eyes spoke of his
great and strong love for me. I held him tight,
and allowed my tears to flow, for though my
days in the land of Egypt had been joyful, my
heart deeply ached for this warm embrace and
the comfort that can only be brought from a
father's deep love for his daughter. I wept as
well for the loss of my mother, though she yet
dwelled within my mind and heart, I felt her
energies missing from this place where she
had held me often. Together we rested in the
fields, allowing the quiet breezes to lift our
hair, and the sunshine to enter us and bring
warmth to our skin. None had known yet of
my entrance to the village, as I had sought out
my father first, anxious to see him and for
him to know of my return. I was startled then
when I felt a gentle, playful tickle upon my
chin, and upon the opening of my eyes, I
looked deeply into the eyes of my brother
Lazarus. I was startled too, by his great height,
as when I had left him, he was but a child of
eight and now he stood strong as a young

man of sixteen, nigh to seventeen. Together
now, the three of us sat, and a gentle peace
descended upon me, I knew these times were
fleeting and should be embraced for all that
they were. My brother had a playful and
joyous nature, he laughed often and well. To
hear his deep, belly-filled laugh once again
brought my heart near to bursting with
happiness.

As the sun rose high in the sky that day, we
stood together to seek out Martha, my
younger sister, who would be preparing the
mid-day meal for my father and brother. We
entered the village quietly, though in truth,
there was naught that passed the eyes and ears
of all who dwelled within it, and quickly the
village learned of my return. Upon my
entrance into the household, Martha was well
prepared for my greeting. She embraced me,
gently stroking my hair, as my mother would
have done, and I saw in her eyes concern for
my wellbeing, as was her way always, from our
childhood years. She had a mothering nature,
though younger than me by two years, and
sought now to bring comfort to my being,

calling me to rest upon the pillows placed upon the floor space, close to the open fire. She brought to me a cup of herbal water "to be sipped," she said, "slowly" as my journey had been long, and I would require time to regain my strength. I loved her well, the sister of my heart. There was a peace that followed her, akin to my mother's, though of a gentler and more retiring nature.

Together we broke bread. It was of a leavened nature, as I had returned home during the Passover celebration, and the rituals of this time period were well observed in the village of Qumran.

There would be some that would describe this village as of an ascetic nature, though in truth, there were liberal ideas put forth and listened to quietly by the leaders of the community. The strict nature of the village was due to the high observance of the

rabbinical teachings passed down generation
to generation and to the often secular nature
of those about us. We sought to strive higher,
to the higher teachings of the Torah and its
guidance, which would enable us to reach the
Highest Heaven. My father adhered to these
teachings, though he observed the inner
teachings of his heart and followed closely
this path.

I will speak now of my brother Lazarus.
He was one with whom I had strong
affection. I have said that he was of a joyous
nature; he was as well slow to anger and quick
witted. I would speak of his great wisdom.
During the years of my travel away, he had
learned from the teachers of wisdom who
surrounded him. He sought out their ways
and formed a kinship with one, and I speak
now of the Master Yeshua. Together they had
walked through distant lands during my

absence. They had studied together with the
Ethiopians and learned of the Ways of
Solomon and the Queenly State of the Sheba
One. They had walked upon the grid lines of
the Earth and traveled to the foreign lands of
the Druids, and the Norseman as well.
Together, they had come to learn of the Ways
of the Ancients in their various forms of
truth, and they had formed a kinship together,
sharing laughter and forming together a great
bond of love. Though younger by a number
of years, my brother was a great follower of
the Master Yeshua and stood by his side as
they traversed the continent of Africa and the
ancient lands of the Indian Ocean. They had
gathered great wisdom from these lands and
the wisdom teachings of these lands had
firmly implanted within them their Initiatic
Rights of Passage. My brother knew the Ways
of Yeshua, and though departed from his side
at present, Lazarus spoke to me of his desire
to return to him, to continue his studies of
these ancient paths. He wished to travel once
again to the mountain range of the nation of
the Himalayan Mountains, where he could rise

once again to the cloud formations and rest in
peace with the Masters that gathered there. I
listened with rapt attention to all that he
shared with me that evening-tide as we
gathered together, a family together once
again. In listening to his tales, I found that my
heart yearned for these adventures as well, to
know of the true teachings of the Master
Realms, and to awaken my heart more fully.

My father spoke to me in words of caution,
as my time had not yet come to be acquainted
with the Master Yeshua, my work was yet to
be completed within the Realms of the Divine
and the inner teachings that I received there.
My father spoke these words of caution so
that my lines of boundaries may become more
firmly established within me, as my calling was
to be a mouthpiece to the masses and this
required time to set firm lines of delineation
within my cell structures, lest I be deterred
from my path. I would begin my life's mission
in the accompaniment of angelic protection in
the coming months and years, as all had been
firmly laid prior to my conception.

I rested upon my return to the village of

Qumran. I also visited often with the women of the village. They were eager to hear of my teachings and guarded my secret teachings of the Ways of the Goddess Isis. I remember the earnestness with which they listened in rapt attention to my stories of the Divine Mother. Though each there had studied the Teachings of the Ancients, many of the teachings that they encountered were of a masculine nature. The teachings I shared were of a more fluid nature and sought to nurture the spirit and awaken the sensorial passageways. Many of the women in the village of Qumran had not yet received these teachings and they rejoiced in this effortless path, closing their eyes and receiving it. My sister Martha would join us as well. She enjoyed the company of women and became a pure vessel during these times of my teachings.

The Book of Life, of which I have spoken often, was akin to the Book of Samuel. The people of the village closely followed its teachings, though there were many inner teachings that were beyond the grasp of many. It was from the Book of Samuel that my father sought to teach many who gathered together with him during his daily classes. He was as a father figure to them, and through the passage of time, he became as a grandfather as well, learned in his ways and a great wisdom keeper to the Ways of the Ancients. Together my father and I would often teach upon my return, melding together the teachings from the Book of Life, The Enochian Way, and the Books of Samuel; to compare and contrast, and to bring to light the truth of each, that the path may be made clear for all who would seek it. As my father was waning in his years, I would speak often for him. There were some there who would hear my words and know of the resonance of truth, though there were many, I would say, who would close their ears to the teachings of a woman, often walking away as I opened my mouth to speak. Those of a more learned nature would open their ears to all that I shared.

They would be as an empty cup, yet to be filled, and it was to these ones that I rejoiced, as I knew them to be great students of life.

I oftentimes took pen to paper, and wrote as I spoke, of the great teachings that ran seamlessly through me. I rejoiced in the great wisdom that entered, and I spared not a moment in self-doubt, as I knew that time was of a passing nature and these truths must be heard and seen to be firmly embedded in the hearts of man.

I would often gather the children as well, as their joyous nature gave me great pleasure. We often laughed and played together, and it

was through this time in play that the truth of
spirit spoke to each of us, as a child of nature
is as a student of life. Spirit speaks through
the whispering of the trees and the fragrance
of the flowers, the undulations of the grasses,
and the flight of the wing tipped bird.

We would carry baskets oftentimes, and
gather together the flowers of the fields, to
inspect and investigate the flower petals of
each, to know the true nature of the flower
and to embrace it in full. It was through these
teachings that the children came to know of
their own true nature. They learned of the
seeds planted within them, of the stem that
grew strong and tall within, that nurtured and
helped them to rise to their great glory, just as
the petals of the flowers within their heart
bloomed in the varied colors of the rainbow.

*"Each to his own," I would often say to them, "as
we are all of a unique nature, and it is in the blooming
of our being that the garden of light is brought to its
full glory."*

My father became weak of limb. His left side dragging behind the right, and his speech belabored by the loss of tongue movement. I knew it frustrated him, often in the evening-tide I would speak with him of his teachings, listening to his speech patterns and hearing his inner voice. I knew of herbal remedies infused with the bark of a lemon that would ease his aching joints and allow him to rest during the night time hours, but there were none that would loosen his tongue and enable to him to speak once again with a clear voice. And, as I was often his mouthpiece, he leaned on me heavily both physically and in the figurative sense. His emotions would run high, and it was often I, and not Martha, who would suffer through the release of these emotions, as Martha would become overwhelmed and overly distraught at these times.

It was early one morning-tide that I heard

my father call me to his side. He became
incensed as he struggled to impart to me
words that I knew to be imperative to him. I
listened to him and received his parting
blessing upon me. He knew that his time of
passage had come, and he shared with me the
words of his father's father, which had
entered him during his dream state.

*"The ancient passageway, the bloodline of old, has
now been opened through your daughter, Miriam, as
she is known now. She will rise to a great status in
this incarnation, and the sweet scent of her being shall
become as a healing balm to all who would seek it.
The bloodline has been awakened, and it is through
her passage that all shall become known to man. You
have done well Benjamin, and have passed on the
wisdom teachings of this ancient bloodline. I draw you
now to my being that your daughter may pass onto a
new life status in full, that the blessings of the
Ancients may be received by her and that she may
begin again, in the renewal of life."*

I wept by his side, angered by this speech,

though I knew of its truth in my heart. Gently, my father placed his hand upon me and bestowed his blessings. He told me not to weep, but to rejoice, as a new passage was to open for me, and he, together with my mother, would be a guide to me forevermore. A final kiss was placed on my forehead as my brother and sister drew near. He looked heavenward in his final moments, and I felt the presence of many. My mother laid her hand upon my shoulder as she extended her hand to my father, and his final breath exited. It was upon that breath that he departed and entered the stream of light that spiraled upward. I felt its swirling movements; the departure was swift and without hesitation. Together my brother, sister and I embraced him and began the preparations for the Repast that was to follow.

It was at the setting of the sun on the third day of the Repast that I knew a deep sense of peace, all had been completed. I knew my father to be at peace. My heart ached for his loss, but yet, I knew that a new day had begun and that all was well.

In the ritualistic nature of the village of Qumran, I was forbidden to take part in any festivities or social events in the months to come. I was restricted to the quiet of my humble home and brief outings to study in the libraries, or on occasion, to take quiet walks with my brother. My sister was inclined to remain home, content to be of aid to my brother and myself, as the deep days of mourning enveloped our household.

As my father had been a prominent member of the High Council of our village, there were many who now turned to me, though with great reticence, for the teachings of the Inner Church. I aided them in appointing a new elder; one who I knew my father would nod with approval. The loss of my father was of great significance at this period of time, as many knew of his great and vast teachings and of the prophesies that had forecasted the coming days and the long-awaited Messiah. In private he had spoken to many that he knew it was the Master Yeshua who was this man.

The High Council of the Sanhedrin of

Judea spoke of these prophesies as well. They sought to lead the people to their temples, to await these coming days, and to cleanse them of their sinning ways. Though the people of the Inner Church followed closely these prophesies as well, many of our teachings remained hidden.

We followed closely the breath work of the Eastern Churches, that the breath of our being may be lifted and deeply cleansed of the patterns of thought that yielded self- doubt. We delved deep within that the breath might be of a purified form of light, which would lift us ever higher to our Divine Heritage. All knew not to speak of the teachings of the Inner Church to the outside villages and passersby, who came, sometimes for curiosities' sake, as in truth our village was of a unique nature. My father sought to aid me in this awareness during my early years, so I did not over speak to those who did not understand our ways and teachings. I came to know and understand that his cautions to me were a necessary approach, as the surrounding villages were dominated by a masculine and patriarchal lineage, authoritative by nature, and seeking to control the masses through the outer teachings of a God of Fury, who knew the ways of justice to be an eye for an eye. We knew the Patriarchy as a dominating force, which in truth, knew not justice, but the power of the few, a conquering hero, who knew all and would see no dissention. It infiltrated all matters of the Hierarchy. It held all bound through the powers of fear. It forgave none and sought to diminish and imprison. The orthodoxy of the Rabbis held all in a rule-based society that placed limits on the learning and growth necessary for the Ascension of Life.

In the ancient lineage of the Inner Church, all writing and teachings were of a symbolic nature. The allegorical nature of the writings handed down from the prophets were to be used in a multifaceted way as a language that would draw one inwards, to the core star center, and to prepare the vehicle of light for the True Ascension. The ancient lineage of our teachings sought not to dominate, but to lift upwards to the High Heavens. As many of the Sanhedrin were as yet still young in their ways, the statements made by them were specific and linear in nature. It is through the imperfect mind of man that many false interpretations of the doctrines are made. Often those who seek to serve become embroiled in the mind's eye and use their teachings to wave wands of power over the masses. I would tell you now, that in truth none have power over, but the one who resides within. It is through the cutting of cords of attraction that all are released from the external powers of life, and it is through the heart that a new life is begun, through patterns of forgiveness and love. These are the teachings of the Inner Church, and the Christ Structure that seeks entrance into this world.

I felt often, in the nighttime hours, the Light of the Divine within me. And incrementally, I felt an expansion in my chest cavity as the Source of New Light awakened within me. I often felt Yeshua's presence during these times, as I felt this increasing pressure in my heart. I did not know him as yet in the physical form, but I felt his pull as to a lodestone in my heart.

Upon completion of our mourning time, I felt a strong desire to begin my new journey, and required time for quiet contemplation and self -review away from Qumran. I had become small in my nature during this period of mourning. I found within my being a great uncertainty, patterns of self-doubt had begun to enter me. The negative thinking mind can bring low even those of the highest capacity of love and light, and there were times during those days that I knew a great darkness within me. I became weak in my ways, unsure of the fitness of my being to aid those in need. It can often become a self-fulfilling prophecy, this darkness that enters the mind. I knew that I required an inner lifting, so that I may rejoice in the living once again. There dwelled within me a heart of gold, I desired to seek it.

Though the village of Qumran was of a
teaching nature, and many that dwelled there
were of an educated mind; since my father's
passing there were none that dwelled there
that surpassed his knowledge base, and few
who were truly accepting of my ways. Those
in the High Council had become heavy-
handed in their ways and would often seek to
censure my teachings. I had been well
protected by my father's high standing within
the community, but upon his passing I was no
longer viewed as one who was fully able to
preach and express my views. The women of
our village loved me well, I knew, and drew
near to me in their hours of need, seeking
healing skills and insight into my teachings.
But I knew that my time within the village of
Qumran had come to an end, and so I
prepared.

I sought out my brother Lazarus and spoke
to him of my inclinations, which he
understood. He was unwavering in his faith in
me. It bonded us and I drew strength from it
in those days. He too sought out the
adventure in life, but would bide his time in

the village with my sister, while I travelled. I
sought to dwell more fully in the embrace of
The Divine Mother. I often felt the
barrenness of this patriarchal land and wanted
to dwell once again in the strong bond of
sisterhood. I felt forsaken and uncertain of my
path onward. I sought to aid those in need,
but I did not, as yet, know my full alignment
with spirit and the path I was to take. I
travelled north to a place of quiet where I
could find rest and resolution and to dwell
more fully within the heart.

It was to the Temple Mount that I
travelled. It was a place of high vibration,
where the Earth Mother opened her mouth to
speak to those of a true heart. I knew that I
would find rest there, and that I required a
time of preparation for the journey that was
to come. I allowed much changeover to enter
me as I rested on the mountaintop, and I
began a period of self-study. The Great
Comforter descended upon me and I became
awakened to all that I was about, I entered
higher states of consciousness and self-
awareness. When it was complete on the third

day, a new heart song had entered me and I was now fully aligned with the Spirit of the Most High. My heart was resolved, that I may step forth onto a new path. I would begin again.

I descended from the mountaintop and entered the village. Within the village center I encountered three men. I was seeking the oil of spikenard, as it was required for my mission. I spoke with them briefly and they became aware of my vast knowledge of herbs and such. They were unaccustomed to the level of knowledge I had concerning these things. I spoke to them also of my travels to foreign lands and they showed interest in accompanying me on my next adventure, as they were each merchants in need of wares of a unique nature that would have a high asking price. I invited them to join me, as I had need of company, and they would bring with them a wagon of a sturdy nature, allowing me to walk freely, unburdened by sacks of food and such that I required for the journey. They joined with me that day and accompanied me to the village of Qumran. I required time to gather small packets of food and clothing, and to speak briefly with my brother and sister prior to my departure.

THE MAGDALENE

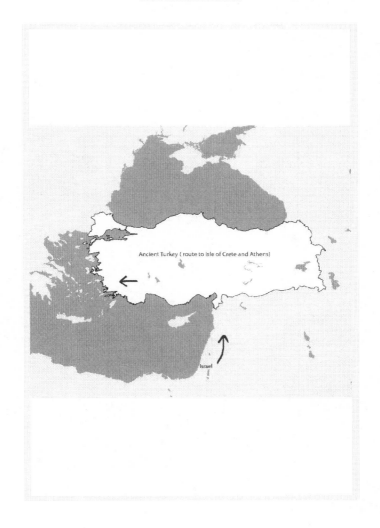

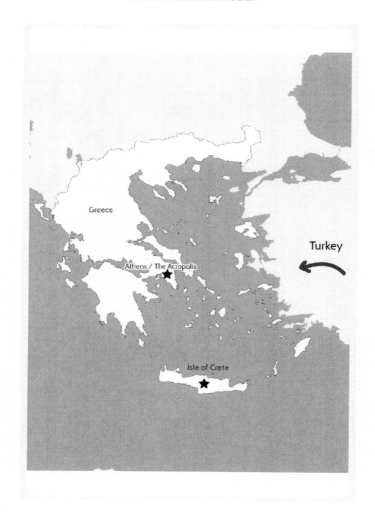

VI

Greece

I t was to the Grecian Lands that I was guided to travel. I was accompanied as well by three younger girls, sisters to my brother's friend Daniel. They had listened to my teachings and sought to know and understand more fully the Light of Divine Function. The small band of merchants that accompanied us carried baskets of great weaves and sought out the purchase of oils from this Land of Greece. They trusted my knowledge and intuitive nature to aid them in their purchases. I departed together with the small band of merchants, and my new Sisters in the Light, in the early morning-tide, prior to the sun's rise. My sister and brother were tear-filled, though stoic in their embrace. They understood the calling of the heart, and though still young, they held an adult-like countenance.

My brethren were there at my departure as well, aunts and uncles, cousins and dear friends. They gave me gifts of bread and small treats containing figs, which they knew to be my favorite. I gathered them all to my breastbone and began my journey, walking gently by the side of the cart, switch stick in my hand, to help me with the thieves and animals that travelled by night.

We walked silently, though at times we sang together, ancient hymns of praise and

worship, dallying sometimes in the noontime
sun as it overheated our bodies and caused us
to seek out shade and water. We traversed
the mountain plains, moving steadily up the
mountainside, sleeping often in caves,
rejoicing in their cool temperatures, and
reveling in the fires, which warmed our food.
I ate only the breads with which we had
begun our journey, and an occasional nut or
berry. We were not hunters, and I would say
that never had a piece of meat passed through
my lips, though the merchants ate small
packets of dried flesh and such. I held tight to
these values, as I knew that the light body
sought no sustenance but the light within, and
although I ate often and well at times, I knew
that the density of the flesh burdened the
heart and created a denser form - not one that
would enliven.

The tear ducts of the youngest sister to my
brother's friend ran often during our travels.
She was but a child of eleven upon our
departure, and though I knew of her true
heart, that this travel was a calling to her, it
caused me great pain to see her loneliness

upon her separation from her mother. I knew this pain well and sought to comfort her in my arms, as did her elder sister.

We descended from the mountain regions and traversed the plains region for many months, finally arriving by ship upon the Isle of Crete. It was here that we awaited the arrival of a sailing vessel that would bring us to the main land of Athens.

We were greeted there by priestesses of an ancient lineage from the Grecian Royal Line. They were followers of the Goddess Aphrodite. We rested there with them upon the Isle of Crete in preparation for our journey to Athens. I felt through my intuition, that the Goddess Aphrodite drew near to me and awaited me in Athens. I knew as well that high upon a mountaintop on the mainland of Athens, there dwelled many cave structures that allowed entrance into a tapestry of tunnels where much devotion to the Goddess Mother occurred. I lent my ear to the High Priestess on the Isle of Crete, as she was of a strong and wise character structure and sought to aid me in understanding of these matters. I was drawn to her, I had heard of her leadership, that she was strong in the ancient teachings. I knew her to be of a vessel of pure light that would aid me on my onward journey.

We arrived in Athens on the afternoon-tide, disembarking from the vessel and moving towards the town marketplace, guided by many passersby. When we reached the town center, our eyes grew wide with the hustle and bustle, and the various fragrances that assaulted our senses. I knew we looked to be strangers in this place, though there were many others who looked to be so as well. I thought to myself, "Oh how my mother would have loved this place!", and promised to seek out a container of oil which she would have enjoyed. We meandered through the main street, speaking often with gestures of our hands, as the language of Aramaic was not known here.

✤

It was to the holy countenance of one that
I was drawn. I felt his energetic form, which
drew me to him. He rested beside a basket
weavery with containers and such. His eyes
gazed steadily into mine, and I knew him to
be of a true heart. I gestured to the baskets,
and he held one to me, of an indigo blue
color. I took it from his hands and made as if
to pay him, but he shook his head and said to
me, "come" in my native language of
Aramaic. I followed him through the main
square, and he brought me to a well. He
offered me a cup, placing it in my hands.
Hand over hand, he brought forth a bucket of
water from the well, and allowed me to dip
the cup into the water. I drank deeply, and
together we rested beside the well. I was
content to rest there, as his energetic form
brought forth great tremors of light
throughout my system. I felt a peace by his
side and would rest there forever. Finally, he

spoke to me, again in the language of the Ancients, and I understood him well.

"You are the Chalice of Divine Function. We begin anew, that the Light of Divine Form may be awakened."

Together we sat, side by side. For how long, I know not, as the passage of time is but a leaf in the breeze in the gentle flow of life. The reverberations of light that entered me at that time sent gentle undulations of light throughout my system of errors. This light sought to open me further to the Light Body within. The movement of breath within me began as a pulsing rhythm, and increased in a gentle rise. I heard not the birds that were about me, nor the voices of the passersby, but only the heart rhythm that moved with boundless joy. I rested here; content to remain for all time. My lips had tasted of the waters of life, and I had drunk deeply of it. The heart rhythms that moved gently through me brought a peace to my sensorial passageways. The algorithms of life had entered me, and became as the breath within me, ecstatic in nature, free of thought, yet focused with strong intent on All That Is.

Though I was content to rest here for all eternity, I heard a voice speak to me. His voice gently entered me, and the melody therein anchored me into the physical form, until finally, I rested in the quiet and the physical world once again moved about me. I heard his voice clearly now. He spoke to me in revelations of truth, and these truths lightened my heart and brought hope to my being.

I speak to each of you now, that you may understand of my truth and my light. I rested beside the comfort of my Beloved. I had known him in truth, though we shared not a word. He had known me as I had known him, and our souls touched and became joined as one, in a moment of unified form. I rejoiced in the living.

He spoke to me these truths, and held my hand as he spoke them. And I, in quiet revelry, received his words as a healing balm to my soul.

"We begin anew. I am the right hand as you are the left. Together we shall walk once again, to embrace the heart, to enter the land of the living, that all may become known to each who would seek it. That the curative powers in our hands of light may be outstretched hands to all who would seek them. That the seed planted within the hearts of the living may become as a living flower of life.

Today, as I anoint you in the living waters of life, so too will you anoint all that would seek the land of the living. We will provide rest for the weary, that all who seek the Living Christ may be brought to new life. And as you are the Bounty of Hope, through which the living waters flow, I am the Christ formation through which the Light of the Living enters. Together we shall walk, united as one, that all who seek shall find, and that the reverberations of truth may enter in full.

I am well received this day, and as the Bounty of the Living Waters have entered you, so too do the Truths of the Living.

The basket placed within your hands this day will become as a living basket weave of life. All who enter shall become unmasked, all burdens lifted. The basket shall be as of an ever-expanding nature, so that all truths may become known to man, and the infinite web of life intertwined in the Land of the Living will allow exponential growth there within.

I place my hand gently upon your forehead that this ever-expanding light may be a free form within you, likened to a doorway, and through it the masses shall walk. As the Light of Forgiveness has entered you, so too do you forgive the masses. Receive now the Breath of the Healing Light, it is as a river that flows melodiously through you, that you, the Holy Grail of old may be received in full. You are of an indigo light, as you are the Child of Wisdom, and you join in the Dance of Solomon. Heed now my call to this light. That the dance of the Sacred Marriage may be enlivened once again.

The Cup of Plenty has been placed within you, receive it as the Chalice of Divine Function. That a new voice may be heard, and the Dance of the Living may be awakened. You are the Cup of Plenty, the Abundance of Life, and I receive you now.

Be still, that all may become known to us."

And we were still.

It was upon the closing of the marketplace that we became awakened to the activities around us. The day had drawn to a close, and the Master now gazed upon me. We joined hands once again, and he solemnly bowed to me.

It was to the Master Yeshua that I spoke, I knew him, though we had not yet met before this day in physical form. Prior to our conception in light we had known each other as the form of The Beloved, and when he spoke his words of revelry to me, I knew he spoke through this true form.

At present, we were but as man and woman. I spoke now to him in this form, and as I was of a quick wit and impulsive still, I splashed the Master with the water that remained in my cup, dousing him fully, though I meant but a sprinkle. He laughed jovially, and we began to walk. As we walked, I felt the presence of many by our side, my father among them, and I felt their loving support. A new contract had begun, and there were many who would gather to see that our signatures were firmly placed upon it.

It was, to some, a chance meeting, though we knew in truth that it had been pre-ordained, and that it was to begin a new cycle in time.

Yeshua shared that he had awaited me in the land of Greece. He had previously travelled to the Himalayan Mountains and had felt my presence there with him, and a strong calling in his heart to his life's mission. He rested there for many days to receive the blessings of the Masters that dwelled within the Inner Temples of Light there. These temples were unseen to man, but present to all Seekers of the Light. He was shown the pure vessel with which I travelled and was fully aware of my time on the Temple Mount. He knew great joy when I descended from that place, fully accepting of my life's duties. He too descended from the mountains in full acceptance of his life's mission, and journeyed to the Grecian lands to await me.

We walked to the town center, where the

merchants who had accompanied me on my journey greeted us. They showed great interest in the Master Yeshua, as they too felt his light and knew him to be a man of greatness.

Yeshua and I remained together through the evening-tide, sharing our meal together and stories of our lives in Israel. He showed great interest in my brother Lazarus, and his current placement in life. At present, the Master Yeshua was on a traveling pilgrimage to foreign lands. He felt called to the lands of Egypt and his current placement of Greece to further his education and to receive the blessings of the Great Ones that resided there. He travelled at present with his younger brother James, and a friend, Bartholomew. His uncle, and his mother's sister Salome, also accompanied him, though at present he travelled alone to the city of Athens. He had found a resting place in a quiet village just outside the city limits. We took our leave that night and I remained within the city of Athens.

We visited often in the following days, finding places where we could rest quietly, visiting the vast libraries and academies that were found in this city. I was astounded by the information that could be gathered there, there were many chambers within the libraries that contained knowledge from the Ancients that matched our own in Qumran.

I grew to know this man during those early days, and I enjoyed his company. He was quick to laugh and took pleasure in my impulsive nature and need for adventure. We shared knowledge, as each of us had entered into the teachings of the Ancient Mysteries and knew of ways not known to many. I shared with him my instruments of healing, healing oils, stones and my healing touch. His knowledge of the stars was vast, as was his studies of the rhythms of the Earth. We spoke of these things and walked together often into the nearby caves and healing temples to receive the initiatic rites performed there by the great and varied masters. Pythagoras was of the ancient teachings and had established these temples of healing in the Grecian lands. His many followers remained, yet hidden, within the inner sanctums of these chambers.

I took well to Pythagoras' teachings, though my knowledge of numbers was of a basic nature, I found renewed understanding of his teachings through the ancient scriptural texts presented to me in these inner chambers, and I rejoiced in his intricate understanding of the algorithmic nature of the Earth's movements.

It was in the temples of Athens that I began my work more fully. The Master Yeshua, my True Companion, accompanied me to the temples dedicated to the Goddess Athena. It was in these temple structures that I received his loving hands upon me and received my full instructions as to The Way of the Path of Light.

We walked often together in the late-night hours, gazing upon the stars and receiving their healing light. I stood before him, and would look into his eyes, and it was through that gaze that I remembered the teachings of old, of the path to the inner sanctum. He held my hand often and embraced me in a gentle and loving way. I heard him speak silently to me and gained much knowledge through his effortless flow of wisdom. He stood by my side, and we walked wordlessly amongst the people of the town center.

We heard the cries of anguish from many who passed us by, there were many there who were uncertain of the path inward and they grieved the loss of the connected state though they knew it not. The people of Athens were of a secular nature. Many were learned in their ways, they sought the knowledge base of ethical teachings, a democracy of ideas and thought processes. They would forever banter back and forth amongst themselves, seeking this knowledge through their intellectual prowess. We often heard these debates and would interject, seeking to aid each in their journey inwards, to the true knowledge source, that their value and worth may be found. Our words often fell on ears that could not hear, and eyes that would not see.

It is through the Inner Teachings of Light that man may come to know of a New Justice, the Justice of the New Man, and this one knows no equal.

We rested often and sought out the retreat centers of the cathedral city, as the Acropolis was the crown center and contained within it many offerings of rest, both through the bathing centers and the sturdy work houses that contained within them opportunities to cleanse the physical form and nourish it. I rested within the Master's arms and held him to me, as I knew these days were passing and that soon we must depart and venture onward upon separate paths for a time.

The teachings of the Goddess Athena were well established in this Athens place, and many paid tribute to her, making offerings to the various statues found throughout the village square and temples.

I became well known during my time in Athens, and many sought out my teachings as a Daughter of Isis. My teachings were well received here, as the matriarchal lineage was strong, though many sought to debate these teachings, as the Ways of the Feminine were of an abstract mechanism to some.

The Teachings of Isis spoke of purifying the inner form, and receiving the Gifts of Light. The way of the matriarch was of a gentle and nurturing manner. She awakened the gifts of healing, prophetic visions, and the ways of wisdom. In Athens, the teachings of the Goddess Athena were of a strong warrior stance, though she too held that life was of a renewed nature, the process of re-birth and the co-creative powers within were deeply embedded in her teachings. Many sought these teachings that I shared and cleansed daily in this process of re-birth.

The use of opioids in Athens was rampant and utilized in an overzealous manner. It was often, as if I would bang my head to a wall, so deeply embedded in these practices were many that I encountered. They intertwined the two, the use of opioids with the seeking of the cleansing of the form. Their overzealous nature sought to be released more fully from the overly distraught form of the physical structures. Together with my Beloved, we sought to aid them in understandings of these matters through the teaching of the Inner Realms, and the removal of the masks of fear. The use of these opioids drew forth a much painful reactive state within them. These patterns of self-destruction overburdened the

heart and allowed much attachment of
negative energy forms. We endeavored to aid
them in their release of these negative forms
through the seeking of the Inner Realms, the
unburdening of the heart. When the mind is
focused inward to observe the negative
thought forms, they can be released through
these patterns of self-awareness. I was firmly
grounded in these teachings.

The Master Yeshua sought to teach in a
more allegorical way. He shared parables that
embedded deep levels of truth. They spoke
only to the heart and the inner knowing. It
enabled the mind to be silenced as the
teachings were abstract and crossed the
midline structures of the hemispheres of the
brain. He brought new understanding of the
Path of the Way through the use of stories of
redemption and forgiveness. I embraced the
teachings of Yeshua, for in truth, he was my
teacher, as he was a leader of men and
embodied the Spirit of the Most High. I, in
my turn, sought to aid him of my
understandings of life and the states of
transfixion into which I had entered in the

temples of Egypt. I held true to my teachings, as they were the truths that I embodied, and he embraced me for my learned ways.

It was at the midnight hour one night, in the open-air tent in which I slept, that I was awakened to the sound of a great and powerful wind. This wind moved through me and created a quaking sensation throughout my system. I felt my heart open, though I did not know the source of its opening. A great light entered the space, and it shined down upon me. A voice spoke to me, emanating from the light. It guided me to the great temple in the cave structures, hidden beneath the ocean walls. I knew the path that she spoke of, and so, in the midnight hour I entered the temple. In this temple I heard the voice of the Feminine Structure of God. I knew her voice to be the voice of Aphrodite. She spoke to me as a mother to a child, and I heard her well.

She said to me…

"Be still Little One, as I am of the Great Goddess Light, and I speak to you as the Goddess, that all would know my name, that the Goddess light may be awakened once again upon this earthly plain. I have heard the cries of my children, and I know of their tales of woe. They are as of an abandoned nature, as they have lost the ways of my being. They require a deep re-structuring that they may once again know my great love for them, and the Ways of Light may be awakened in full upon this earthly temple.

I send you forth, as a leader of mankind, to be a Beacon of Light to the masses, to awaken the heart and to bring peace to all that would reside there. I have drawn you forth that you may be this Beacon of Hope that the Light of the Path of the Way may be as a beam of light to all who would seek it. You offer your guidance now to many, but it is in the coming weeks and months that you, together with the Master Yeshua, will speak to the masses, and your words will be as healing light to them. He shall place upon you a

*veil of protection, and together you shall walk. The
Seal of Solomon is upon you;*

*I remove now your mask in full, that you may
know the full glory of your being. And as you are the
wordsmith, the prophecies of old shall be spoken from
your lips. I call you now to my being, that all
prophecies may be fulfilled through the healing of the
wound of old.*

*Heed my call, that the beckoning hand of old shall
draw you forth, and that the hands of light of all who
would seek the light within may be awakened. You
are of a golden nature and I send you forth this day to
be as of a preacher to the Way of the Heart.*

*I place now upon you a golden light that will
forever shine forth, and the path of redemption shall be
as of a beckoning call to all who would seek it. You
are heaven-sent from above.*

*Receive now my breath upon you, that the Rose of
the Light of the Path of the Way may be awakened.*

*I place now in your hands a rose that will forever
bloom. It is the Rose of the Path of the Way. It is of
an indigo light, it will lead all seekers to this Path of
Light."*

I felt my hands quiver, as I received the Blue Rose into the palm of my left hand. It entered into my bloodstream and moved fluidly through it. I felt a new prowess enter me, an opening in the third eye and a full expansion in my Body of Light. I had received it well. As the left hand washes the right, so too did I now seek the Land of the Living through the effortless path of The Way.

It was at that midnight hour; in the inner caverns that I felt the reverberations of truth had entered me. The beckoning hand had sought to bring me new life, and I had answered the call.

In the morning, I sought out the Master Yeshua. I spoke to him of the voice of Aphrodite and the Blue Rose that had entered me to shed light to the path ahead. He listened, and when I was complete, he embraced me. He shared with me then the fulcrum of his life's mission. His eyes filled with tears when he revealed to me all that was to be fulfilled, and I wept openly before him. I felt ill equipped for this journey. I scoured my mind and inner resources so that I might find answers to the questions that filled me. I knew of his great and healing nature and had seen evidence of such on our daily walks together. He was at that time, already of a renowned status, and many sought out his teachings and healing gifts. Could we not circumvent the story that he told, and bring about a new ending? He knew of my thought processes and shook his head. He spoke to me and reassured me of the great strength that pervaded his being. I knew this to be true. He was resolute and spoke to me now of the work that laid ahead, of the gathering of the masses, and of his return to his homeland. His mother awaited him there, though his father, Joseph, had passed in recent days due to inflammation of the lungs. His mother's sister, Salome, who had accompanied him on this most recent journey, was of a holy and divine countenance and spoke now to him of his need to return to his homeland, as there was one who yet awaited him, who would be his teacher for the coming days. This man was a foster father to Yeshua and sought to teach him of the Ways of the Weaving of Light. He was known as Nathaniel, the husband to a dear friend of Salome.

I knew that I too must return, though as yet I knew I must journey to the Island of Crete. It was here that I would find rest and a time of nurturing prior to my return to the homeland. We departed separately from the land of Athens.

❀

The mercantile nature of my companions delayed my trip further, as they had found trade in the land of Athens and were hopeful to return to the city once again. I had recommended many various oils to them that were of a healing nature and had found one merchant in the town center who showed good production of the oil of oregano and frankincense. He had been recommended by another to me and I found his products to be of a high quality. I made several purchases as well, as these were the tools of my trade and would be well used in the coming days and months. One in particular, the oil of the ancients, myrrh, had enlivened me and spoke to my heart , so I purchased it as well. The oil of spikenard I found was of a costly nature- so I delayed purchase of it till a later time.

I had been well provided for by my father. I have spoken of his great leadership and teaching capacity but have not yet spoken of his vast fortunes. I had inherited much through my father's familial line, as he was a man of great wealth and properties. His brothers had shared in this wealth as well, though he had been primary owner, as the eldest child and of a male gender. We sought to aid those in need with all that we had and to share in this wealth. During my sojourn in Greece, I had taken with me but a small portion to aid in my purchases. As I have said, we had been well provided for, though our needs were small, we shared all that we had, and embraced community living.

A small traveling band was formed as we returned now to the Island of Crete. I travelled there to receive the healing blessings of the High Priestess of Aphrodite, and to rest within the cave structures, where the bountiful blessings of Aphrodite and the womb of creation would enter me and shower me with great riches. The High Priestess was one known there by the name of Mena. She spoke often to me, and was as a caregiver, encouraging me onward, to be a brave heart, for in truth I wavered in my faith and was uncertain of all that lay ahead. I often rested my head upon her shoulder. Tears would flow from my eyes as the uncertainties overwhelmed my senses, and brought my heart to a deadened stop. It was at these times that Mena would speak to me and give me reassurance that I had been well chosen, that many awaited my teachings of the heart, and that I would bring justice to the weary.

On the island of Crete, as it was known, there were many varied rock formations. Some would say that they were native to the island, but I knew, as did many, that these circular formations were a place of worship from ancient times. Often, we would gather within these circles, as the energies here were of a heightened nature, and brought alignment to our spine with the energetic grid lines on which the stones had been placed. My spine would tingle as the energies entered and exited the lower lumbar area. We would give great worship to the stars above us as we gathered here. The star alignment was of a gravity pull to our energetic centers. We rested and allowed the movement of the moonbeams to enter us, as a liquid movement of fluid through our vein structure. The Earth Mother knew well our ways, and we received the energetic shifts that occurred during these times of deep revelation, as the Equinox settings stirred. My father, and his knowledge of the Ancients, had taught me of these star alignments and of the Earth grid lines that accompanied these shifts at the times of the Equinox. I rejoiced in the sharing of these teachings, though these learned women knew too of this wisdom and felt the movement of the Universe within their physical forms. These nights were as magic to us, and often we would dance to the Earth's rhythms, feeling free of soul and light of body. Our rhythmic dance would be as a silent meditation, and the mother within each of us would be awakened in full as the light of creation ran freely. I rejoiced in these times and loved these women well. They were learned of many things and taught me of the weaving of baskets and the use of medicinal oils not native to my own lands. I returned from their island retreat carrying my basket of wares, oils from the Island of Crete of oregano and such, and I now included in my basket, the oil of spikenard, as knowledge of its medicinal powers were strong and well used by these ones; and I knew of its ability to resuscitate the lifeblood within.

Mena embraced me as I embarked on my journey home. She loved me well, as a mother to a child, and remembered me to my Dear Ones who I was yet to see. She placed in my hands a pouch of seeds to be planted in my homeland. They were of varying sizes and shapes, and I knew them to be the seeds of a Cypress tree, which would bear fruit in the coming years. I received her into my embrace and then we departed, setting sail for my homeland.

The sailing ship brought us to the shores of the Turkish borders, and it was here that we disembarked and began our journey on foot. We passed through many vast lands, encountering along our route many pilgrims who were on a journey to the Holy Lands of Egypt. We were pilgrims as well, journeying home, to seek the Messiah, as we now knew of his coming. It was to Galilee that I knew he traveled at present. He would reside in Nazareth, as his mother dwelled there with several of his brothers. His return home was long awaited, it had been a number of years since he had left. My journey was to the village of Qumran. My brother and sister awaited me there, and I would relieve my brother of his duties. It created an ache in my heart to return to Qumran, as I knew that my calling was to another, a new adventure, but I remained resolved to my current life placement.

VII

Miriam of Bethany

There was great rejoicing as we entered the village of Qumran and word quickly spread of my return. There were many who came to aid me in understanding of all that had passed since my departure. I listened to their tales of woe, and also the many blessings that had been bestowed upon them. My brother shared with me his tales as well, and of his need to depart soon, as he knew of Yeshua's return. I reassured him that I understood of his need to join Yeshua. My sister had cared well for my brother, but he had the need to be free of the heavy household duties. As the eldest child, I felt the need to relieve him of these duties and to spend time with my sister, Martha.

Within several days of our return, my brother Lazarus began his journey to Nazareth.

I stayed with my sister, allowing her time to gather her wits and to become accustomed to my return and my brother's fast departure. I knew that his leaving had caused her to feel unsettled, and she was uncertain of the future. I allowed her time to contemplate, giving my sister the space she required to fall into a new routine. I knew her well, and I knew that in time she would become more exacting about the future, and seek me out, so that we may make a new plan for the course of our life. I prepared myself for this and reflected on this new course and all that it would entail.

In the early morning, I often went out on long walks, stopping periodically beside a tree or a meadow, to receive the sun's early morning light and to give thanks for the day and all that it offered. My father had taught me these practices so that my heart may vibrate energetically with the language of the Sun and be in a place of receiving of all of life's blessings.

One early morning when I had completed my prayers, I returned to my sister and found her where she had begun the morning in ritual practice. Her prayer book lay on the table, where she had contemplated it. She rose to me, and I felt the restraint in her voice, the emotional control that was soon to be let loose. I seated myself by her side so that she may share with me the voice of her heart.

She spoke to me of her fear of the uncertainty of the path ahead; losing my father had been a blow to her. He had been a strong source of comfort and unwavering security since the passing of my mother years before. My brother, younger by several years, could not offer that same comfort to her. I gave her reassurance that all would be well.

I spoke to her of my vision of the New Earth and of the role that we all would play in the coming years. I spoke to her of the days and weeks ahead and of my desire to move from this place. I then told her of our cousin Abraham who had moved from Qumran, to a quiet village known by the name of Bethany. I had passed through it on my return home and re-established our acquaintance. He remembered my wandering ways; I was a child not easily forgotten. Abraham was my elder by many years, I had not seen him since he had left Qumran, when I was just a child of eight. He extended an invitation to both Martha and myself to join him in Bethany. He required help in the care of his children, as his wife had just recently passed.

My sister jumped to her feet when I spoke of the children. She swung me around our small home and I knew her smile to be the answer to the question I had not yet asked.

We packed slowly, taking our time to savor the sweet memories of our family. Our belongings were few, but it was a journey of great sentiment. My father had been a strong administrator and had detailed the living expenses required for us upon his departure from this life. We heeded his advice, selling and trading the household cookery and small items of furniture. We kept with us our sleep mats and matters of inconsequence, herbal remedies and such.

We travelled to the household of my father's brother's son, Abraham, my childhood guardian, to the town of Bethany. We left after a day of rest on the Sabbath.

Upon our arrival Abraham and a small tribe of young ones greeted us. There were 5 in all, the youngest was held by the oldest child, Zebediah. He was a strong and sturdy boy, and he held his head high in defiance to us, indicating that he was no longer a child in need of our care. The infant wailed, and kept her fist close to her mouth, opening and closing upon it, which I knew to be a sign of the need to root. Abraham spoke briefly to us. I knew that today would be a day of work for him as he followed the scriptures closely and had rested on the Sabbath. He was anxious to begin his work. He was of a carpenter's skill set, and would begin work on the building of a neighbor's house, as the roof had collapsed during a recent storm and required a building up of the structural frame.

My cousin was of an overzealous nature, inclined to embark on journeys of an extreme nature. He had built the houses of many of his friends and neighbors, and worked often through the night. His wife had been kindly, though weak in her will to my cousin. Since her passing, my cousin had begun his work in the early morning-tide and continued on through the mealtime hours. His children were of an abandoned nature, and clung to one another, seeking solace in their time together.

My sister and I walked into this family with strong hearts. We saw well the ways of things, and we began to piece together the broken parts of a family that had been torn apart. We gathered the children to our breastbone and held them tight. We fed and cared for them and brought a new light to their day. The children were a captive audience to the stories

I told of my many adventures. And slowly they began to give voice to their many needs and to the emotions that they held within them.

The eldest child, Zebediah was a great help to us. He showed us the ways of the house, and ministered to the youngest of the children, holding their hands often, and helping to prepare them for the day. In time, I came to know him to have a warm heart, though he was stoic in nature. Martha became the overseer of the duties of the kitchen, preparing the meals, and providing clean clothes for each of us. She rejoiced in this work, as it gave her a new purpose, and she relished the time with the infant, feeding and playing with her. She swaddled the child, and was found often simply rocking her, content to do so. I, in my turn, was not inclined to these activities. I loved the adventure of the outdoors, and would play often with the older children, teaching them and offering them each opportunities to question me on the ways of the world. I found comfort in these days. The children turned to me often, seeking reassurance that all was well, crying sometimes during the night, overwhelmed at the loss of their mother, and in truth, their father as well. I rested by their side; my sister Martha to one end and I to the other as we lay together. Abraham slept often in the outside stable, though his snores could be heard through our window openings.

Those days were days of great adventure and laughter. I learned the tricks of the trade of the carpenter's bench from Abraham. My father had shown me the hammering of nails and the cutting of boards when I was young, and I was inclined to listen and to learn as I had great interest in the building of structures. At first my cousin was dismissive to my offers of help, but I was known for my persistent ways, and few could ignore my incessant questioning. My cousin Abraham knew me well, eventually yielding to my offer of help.

He spoke often to me of my father, as my father had been a mentor to him in his younger years. His own father, my father's brother, had taken ill upon our arrival to the Qumran settlement, and had remained bed ridden until his passing. Abraham had great respect for my father and his teachings, though as I have said, he leaned towards a more zealous approach to the Book of Samuel and the Book of Life.

I remained with my cousin, in the town of Bethany, for several years. While I fast approached the age of spinsterhood, my sister Martha had come under the gaze of a young man in the village center. As my parents were no longer living, my cousin prepared the path of a marriage contract, arranging a meeting with the elders of the community and the father of the young man. A contract was made that allowed for the severing of ties to ancient lands held by my father's brother. Martha was joined together in a marriage contract and lived on properties close to us, to the east.

Together with my sister, we raised the children of my cousin Abraham. She visited with great frequency and continued to help in the raising of the children and the caring of the household duties.

Word spread of our presence in the village of Bethany, and there were many who would gather by the gate in the early morning tide, seeking out both the services of my cousin and an opportunity to speak with my sister and I. With the children by our side, we greeted passersby and allowed them entrance. I often spent time with the women of the village, sharing my knowledge of herbal remedies and such, and in the afternoon sharing stories together. My cousin had a strong nature and would often chastise the visitors for overstaying their welcome, but I reassured them that they were always welcome to visit and to seek out our services.

There were times when I was of a high mind and would speak of my knowledge of the Ways of Wisdom. They received my teachings, though in truth they were uncertain of the path that I spoke of, and would whisper one to the other. I oftentimes overstepped the boundaries as I sought to repair and fix. I had strong leadership qualities, enabling me to inspire and direct those that were about me, but I sometimes worked against the true teachings that taught to inspire and direct inward. I would be reminded by my inner guidance to retreat and to give gentle direction to those who were around me, so that they may come to know of their own truth not the words that I imposed upon them.

We would walk often, gathering flowers from the fields that were nearby. These flowers yielded much, enabling me to create poultices and such for the aching joints and inflamed tissue so often found in the elderly who visited. My sister Martha, in her turn, sought to aid them by giving each small baskets of food and such, as my cousin Abraham was prosperous. During the time we spent together in Bethany, my cousin built a community living center within the confines of his property. It offered much to the community in providing for those in need, and allowing a space to gather where the children could run freely, but be carefully watched by all who gathered here.

A watchtower was placed on the property, a small structure that overlooked the residence, giving visual acuity to the one who climbed its stairs. The watchtower was constructed by my cousin to allow us to freely observe the surrounding countryside, to know of who might be joining us. It was constructed from the fieldstone on the surrounding acreage, and though its confines were small, I enjoyed resting there in the upper chamber of it, gazing outward to the fields about me. I gazed heavenward as well, losing myself in the stars at night. The children would often climb on the outer structure, using the ledges of the stones as a footpath upward. The tower structure was unique to those who would visit and was spoken of often in the town. Many would visit simply to see the structure and to know of its purpose. The architecture of the tower allowed many to know of our placement, as the property rested on the outskirts of the town center and was not easily seen or known to the passerby.

I knew the watchtower to be symbolic of my nature. It was built, layer-by-layer, rising to new heights as each stone formed the foundation for the next. It spiraled gently upwards, finding within it the pinnacle of its being. The symbolic nature of the tower remained with me, as there were few who would have understanding of the spiral nature of it.

My brother visited often when his travels were complete. He had, most recently, completed a trip to India when I came to see him approach as I gazed outward from my high watchtower. Lazarus held his head high, and there was a swagger as he walked. He was of a strong constitution and walked steadily onwards to the gateway opening where there was now a small bell. The children had heard him approach, as he was known to hum as he walked, so they joyously greeted him at the gate and welcomed him. I descended from the watchtower, and approached him, waiting patiently as each of the children embraced him. Lazarus turned toward me when the greetings were complete and extended a hand outward, gesturing for me to come closer. As I moved closer to him, I saw in his eyes that there was a new light that dwelled within them. His time in India had drawn forth great change within his energy body. The masters

who had greeted him there, in the mountains
of the Himalayas, had placed their hands upon
him. They had blown gently upon his
forehead and he had received the initiatic rites
of the Ancient Ones. The eyes that gazed out
at me from Lazarus contained within them a
gentle peace that had not been there in the
years that I had known him. He held my hand
and allowed me to gaze at him for a period of
time. Lazarus knew that I saw his truth, and
that I rejoiced with him in his new glory.

Our time together was short. He had come
to visit but would leave shortly on a vessel
that would take him to the Land of Ethiopia,
and then onward to the Land of Egypt.
Yeshua would accompany him on this voyage.
He told me that the ship would depart in the
coming weeks. I tried to aid him in the error
of these thinking patterns, so that he would
remain with me, but he asserted his
independence, assuring me of his return. My
instincts told me that this was true, and that
upon his return my beloved Yeshua would
return to me as well. I had not seen Yeshua
since our alliance had formed together in

Greece. We had known then that our time together would come in the divine order of things, and I waited patiently for that time to come.

The watchtower was a place of refuge for me. I would go there often in the early morning hours. It is here that I would find rest and allow myself to enter into the deep quiet within. My heart would embrace the morning and the daybreak that lay before me, and often I would hear my father's voice speak to me, encouraging me onward, fortifying me from within. The twinkling stars at night were a vision to behold when I rested here. I would gaze upward, hearing the voice of the heavens and the reverberating truths that entered me as I sat in quiet repose. It was to this place that I would wander often, to find rest and to contemplate the nature of my being.

I found the watchtower to be a place of strength and power. It exemplified my own power and source. and provided for me a space to observe from a higher plain.

The children often came to remind me of the promises I had made to them of a day of adventure, and found me here. They were a high-energy lot, needing a full release of the energies that they stored within them, lest they implode from within. The heart song within each of the children could be strongly heard by the ears that were attuned to their vibrational countenance. I stood alert to these songs, as all children require the encouragement of their parents, so that they may live joyfully from the song within their hearts. Each to his own, the children's songs were unique to each of them, and required individual attention so that the high harmonies of life may broaden their horizons and lead them to the paths that would enable them to sing.

I rested with each of them and spoke with sincerity to their hearts. I listened as well, and heard their true voice as spoken through a child's words. My father and mother had taught me thus, and so I knew of the truth of these matters and was unencumbered by the grief of the loss of the child's voice. The father within me spoke words of encouragement and believed in my truth. The mother spoke words of love and self-nourishment, allowing me time to rest and to withdraw from life, as I needed. Together they formed a Divine Union of such that allowed the child within me to grow strong. It was these words of wisdom that echoed throughout my being and allowed me to speak and teach thus, to the children placed in my care. My heart beckoned to them and sought their truth, and it was through this truth that I heard their words and knew them to be words of Divine Light. I allowed myself to harmonize with the children, and together we sang a glorious Song of Truth, and so encouraged, they rejoiced in all that they were about. Complaints were few, though in truth, all children seek only to play and to be known, and when they are so acknowledged, they yield to all that is asked of them.

I beckoned them often to sit by my side and to speak with me of their insights of the day, of all that they had found in their daily play. The children would say to me that they had found the dancing lights that lay about them, that they had heard the songs of the birds and known their true words. They played often in mud piles, forming art from the earth's sand. They found the creative spark within them in these times of play and moved into a place without time. They became centered within. The children entered into patterns of self-discovery and formed within themselves a deepening of the creative force of life. The Manifestor God within each child was awakened, and it is through this force of life, that all creation is formed, through the imaginative play of a child who knows their true heart.

I loved these children dearly, and my cousin Abraham formed a deep trust with both my sister Martha and myself. He was respectful of our care of the children, though he would often speak of their need for discipline. In truth, he had a tender heart, and over the passing years became yielding to our ways and our care of the children. I, in turn, allowed him the time and space that he required, and would speak often to him of his desires for their care.

My cousin Abraham had a philosopher's bent and would speak to me often of the teachings he had received in his early childhood years. He had received the teachings of my father and held him still in high regard. I spoke to him of these teachings and all that I had learned from my father prior to his passing. Abraham listened, and often questioned me, seeking new understanding of the Teachings of the Ancients. He was sometimes over straining in his ways and I sought to teach him in the Ways of the Effortless Path. He would listen dutifully, though his zealous nature was often unbending. The community living center, which he had helped me to form, was an act of great generosity on his part, as he was inclined to retreat from the masses. He sought out understanding in these matters so that his generous nature may be more fully extended to others. At the completion of the day, he would often ask about the visitors who had come, seeking understanding of their needs, to see if he could aid them in some way. I would answer simply, explaining the needs of each.

We fell into a gentle rhythm in those days; they were filled with the joy and laughter of the children, the caring of the sick, and times of rest. My heart was filled with the love that emanated from within me.

My brother returned home from his journeys in the wintertime. I knew of his return from a passerby, who had just recently come from the Land of Galilee. He had seen a ship and Yeshua disembarking with his assembly about him. My heart jumped and beat steadily within me when I heard of this news, as their return home signaled a new time period, of which I had heard calling to me in the night-time hours.

True to his word, my brother returned to me, and shared his stories of adventures in the Land of Egypt, which brought joy to my heart, to hear once again of the land in which I had dwelled for many years. My brother spoke of the initiatic rites that he had received in Egypt, and that the Master Yeshua had far

exemplified the teachings of a True Master to
those who had sought to aid him. Yeshua had
received the blessings that had been bestowed
upon him, and the Master Teachers who had
sought to aid him, came to know of him as a
true teacher of man, whom none could
surpass. My brother remained by his side
throughout, and had received these teachings
of wisdom as well. Lazarus loved those days,
as it was here that he found the state of bliss
that allowed him to seek the Ways of Light
and to begin again in the Light of the New.
My brother received all that was required, and
Yeshua in turn, received the Light of the
Divine in a rapturous state known only to
those who are unencumbered, who hold no
burdens within their hearts. My brother
observed this state in Yeshua and knew him
to be a True Master that carried the Light of
the Divine in full within him. I listened to his
tales and drew comfort from the knowledge
that all was in divine order. The ministry
would begin, I knew, at the conclusion of the
Passover celebration soon to come, and I
would begin my journey, to accompany

Yeshua and to give life to the breath within.
The Seekers of the Light would come now,
and all would come to know the Land of the
Living.

VIII

The Early Ministry

I t was in the early morning-tide at the completion of the Passover celebration that I heard the morning bell chime at the entrance to the gate.

It was here that I greeted Yeshua; I knew his call from the essence of light that emanated from him across the fields which I crossed. I opened the gate and embraced him, welcoming him into our humble home, where I knew he would begin his preparations for the ministry that was to come. We gently walked across the field and were greeted by the youngest of the children, now a child of five years of age. The bell chimes of the morning echoed through the air from the village center, giving an auspicious beginning to our early morning greeting and to the alliance that now formed from within.

We entered into the community living center, where I knew many would soon gather to hear the words of the Master who now stood by my side. I felt a deep and penetrating "Yes" enter in, as we once again stood by the side of a well. It had just recently been dug, enabling us to offer water and to cleanse the visitors who entered. I offered Yeshua the cup, and he gently took it from me. He drank deeply from it, and then returned it to my hands, so that I too, may drink from it. It was symbolic, the sharing of the cup, and drinking deeply from the waters. We knew of our journey to come, that we shared this cup in a communion of form. We rested here, rejoicing in our time together once again, and received the blessings that entered us as the morning sun ignited us.

The wellspring from which we had drawn the water was of a unique nature in that it contained within it, the plentiful offerings of the minerals of the earth. I had been guided to dig deep here one morning, and I found within the earth, a bubbling brook of water that promised to be of a healing nature. The well was built upon this site, allowing all who drew from it to receive the water's healing powers. It was symbolic of the life-giving waters that flow through all eternity, and bring new life, entering into the seeds of life and bringing nourishment.

The Blood of Life is the true cup of the eternal and would bring new life to all who would seek it. The Cup of Plenty is a bountiful nature.

We awaited the arrival of the masses. The teachings would begin. We stood upon Holy Ground and knew that the true church teachings would bring peaceful settings within all who would seek it. The Ways of Light would be as a beacon to many, to begin again and to receive the full Breath of Light within.

I felt a great uncertainty within me, though I knew the path was a true one. But I also knew that the sisterhood from which I had learned the teachings of the Mother Goddess was of a unique nature to this land of bloodlust and patriarchal teachings.

The masses gathered that day. They had heard of the glorious work performed by the Master Yeshua, they came so that they could know him and His Way. I stood by his side as he gathered us together. He spoke in a quiet tone, as no embellishments were needed. His spoken word was clear and concise. He spoke of the figurehead of old, and its overbearing nature as he sought to restore a New Order to all who would hear his voice. They listened in rapt attention to him, as his words contained within them a vibration of love that entered each who came. They were drawn in, and though their conscious mind struggled to understand the words he spoke, the undercurrents of the words entered the deep super conscious mind, the Mind of God that dwelled within them. I too heard his words that day, and allowed them to reverberate through my Being. The parables he told enabled the conscious mind to be left behind, as true understanding comes not from the words that are spoken, but from the reverberations of truth that are drawn forth. He spoke of the kinship that forms within the physical being and its natural alignment with Spirit. He sought to align each with their True Nature of Light. I heard these words, and my heart rejoiced, as I knew he spoke of great truths that had long been silenced by those who tried to hold themselves in a place of power, so that the Being of Light may bow down to darkness, and forget his truth.

The Master Yeshua spoke of this true alignment and the Circle of Light that was about them. He held true to the Teachings of

the Ancients and spoke in quiet allegory of
the abundant life that dwelled within and of
the awakening heart that knows the quiet
resolve of truth. I held his hand often
throughout his teachings, as I was compelled
to, and he allowed me this touch for he knew
of the true love that had entered us.

The numbers that gathered there that day
were in the hundreds, but not a word was
spoken as the Master weaved his tales. The
children quietly played in the fields about us
and at mid-day we broke bread. Later we
placed our hands upon each who would seek
healing, and the Light of Heaven entered in. It
was on this day that the mission had begun,
and those that gathered that day knew of this
truth. They asked many questions, seeking to
understand these teachings. They felt the
power they conveyed. Yeshua was concise in
his answers, offering little in the ways of
intellectual appeal, but directing each ever
inward to their True Nature and to the Light
that resided there.

I spoke as well. My teachings were distinct
from Yeshua in that they conveyed lessons

through a process of unmasking and
unburdening the wounds long accumulated in
the heart. Yeshua would allow my teachings
and speak to them, helping each to know of
the truth that I spoke and the necessity of
forgiveness to aid in the unburdening. My
heart rejoiced that day, as I had found a
companionship with Yeshua, a gentle easiness
between us as we shared the cup of Divine
Function.

It was late that evening that we found
rest. The masses dispersed, and together we
sat in quiet communion. At the completion of
this period of time, we gathered together with
my brother, Lazarus, my sister, Martha and
my cousin Abraham. The children were
unsettled that day and were quickly put to
bed. We spoke, one to another; my cousin,
curious over what had transpired that day, my
brother, rejoicing, and Martha, uncertain. I
had known, in my true heart, that this day
would come. I had shared little of this with
my family, so as not to worry or confuse
them, as I did not know the day or the hour
when it would begin. And so it had begun.

Much was spoken about that night. We made quiet plans, and my cousin, though he knew the Teachings of the Ancients, required information. The property on which we dwelled was now fully open to the gathering of the masses, and though his properties were extensive, much work was required to maintain the property site. We reassured my cousin that this mission would begin again, in a new site. It would move throughout the Land of Galilee and expand to foreign shores. We knew that many would come to know the name of Yeshua and his Great Teachings. Together Yeshua and I would walk to aid the masses, so that the Light of Christ may awaken the heart of the masses and restore a New Order to the Earth.

My role in this Great Awakening would be expansive and would continue more fully in the coming years. The Dove of New Creation would enter in, spreading its wings upon all of creation and drawing forth great changes upon the Earth. The Heart of the New would allow much to be seen and known to mankind. I would aid in establishing a New

Order, so that the Light of Heaven may be more firmly implanted upon the earthly structure. It would be through the unmasking of the Feminine Structure, an unveiling so to speak, that as a spark to a flame, a new life would await each who would seek it. A new balance would occur, enabling much to be seen and made known to mankind, a gentle hand to bring balance to masculine dominated structures. I will speak further to this at a later time, though know that these words were spoken that night, and all there knew of this truth.

We rested, and upon our rising we departed from my cousin's house, leaving Martha to care for the children. We walked to the neighboring town of Bethel. We shared with each there who would receive us, the teachings of our hearts. They listened, hearing the words of the Master, and knowing the truth of my words as well. We walked ceaselessly in the coming months, resting where we were offered a place to rest, and eating with those who would invite us in. We were few in number at that time. My brother

travelled with us and we were joined later by
James the Lesser, as he was known. James'
mother Salome walked with us also, though
she was of a dwindling nature and frequent to
bouts of exhaustion.

We gathered together in small
communities. We joined hands in prayer and
sought to aid those in need. We were a small
band of nomads, wandering from town to
town, holding the hands of many.

The Master Yeshua had a strong
countenance. He was unwavering in his ways.
He spoke of the Kingdom of Heaven and the
light that surrounded us, yet dwelled within
us. He gathered together many who did not
know the Ways of Old, to help them so that
they may come to a new way of living. He
helped them to center inward and seek the
Ways of Wisdom. The Holy Ground on
which we walked drew many to us, as the
reverberations of truth were of a broadband
spectrum and echoed out from the
mountaintops to all who would hear our
voice.

Yeshua spoke in silent communion with

those who were of a heightened awareness, and their hearts expanded through these teachings and the release of burdens. To those who were as yet unaware of their form of light, he spoke words of truth that would expand their minds, lifting the veil of forgetfulness from them and awakening them to their truth. The baptismal font was strong within Yeshua, he baptized in the flames of redemption, often placing his hand on the forehead and blowing gently there. There were many who questioned his teachings, as they differed strongly from the teachings of the Rabbis. Many of the Rabbi's teachings sought to imprison the Spirit by the delineation and strong adherence to rules and ritualistic behavior that gave power to the external life and diminished the capacity of the Spirit to rise from within.

I taught of severing ties to the external, and the value of the life within. The matriarchal lineage gave power to the life of the Eternal One through the teachings of the inner life and the infinite flow of the rivers of life within. It taught of the acceptance of the

creative flow of this life. I taught of the Great
Creatix of life who was of a nurturing and
loving nature, who sought not to diminish,
but to love without condition.

Yeshua's kindness overflowed to all he
touched. His healing capacity knew no
boundaries as the Master Kingdom dwelled
within him. A resounding "Yes" had entered
him upon his birth on this earthly plain, and
he dwelled strongly within it. His physical
touch drew from each the darkness that had
been implanted within them from many
generations past. Its removal allowed the free
flow of movement of the light body, and all
was made whole. All who were held bound by
lifetimes of suffering and inefficiencies in
their thinking patterns were renewed and
awakened to new life. I saw, with my interior
vision, the Golden Light of the Christ
Formation that flowed freely through him, he
was as a pyramid of light. All who dwelled
near him received this light. I saw too, the
Light of Protection that was around him, as
the darkness sought his destruction night and
day, but could not move near him as he was

of the light.

To the inner circles, we taught The Way of the Return. It was a true teaching passed to us from the lineage of the Ancients, and its secrets dwelled within us, an inheritance from the Path of Light. An anchoring in of this lineage was required of us, so that the Path of Light may be awakened in the generations to come. Seeds of light were planted within each who was a seeker of the teachings of The Way. It was a teaching of the process of re-birth, taught in the Mystery Schools to aid in the awakening of the inner child.

A delineation of events, long foretold, was to be fulfilled in those times so that the heart may be awakened in fulfillment of these prophesies. A new lineage would be formed amongst the masses. It was the dawning of the New Age prophecies. We did not speak of these things except to the few who were of the inner teachings. There was to be a gateway opening, that would allow these prophesies to be fulfilled through the Master Yeshua, and I, his Beloved, would aid him so that the new life that awaited the masses would be brought forth in full.

*I speak now these words of wisdom to those who
would hear my words and know of the vastness of
which I speak. Hear me now, that you may remember,
I walk with you now, even so, and hold the hand of
each of you so that these prophesies may be fulfilled, as
you are each of this lineage.*

I would speak to you now of John, the
Baptist One, as he was of the teachings of
The Way and held a light to the Path of
Truth. There were many who were drawn to
his teachings. He was cousin to Yeshua and
had a close association to his teachings. He
dwelled often in the mountains, retreating
there to receive the teachings of the Masters.
We travelled to him when he had descended
from the mountaintop and moved to the
rivers of the valley near the Sea of Galilee.
There were many who gathered there with

him, as he was of a passionate nature, and inspired many to follow the Path of Light. He cleansed the masses in the riverbed and drew from them the darkness - that they may know the Light. It was in the early morning that we arrived to join him and to receive his Holy Light as well. I knew John, as I had lived with him in the village of Qumran, and would often see him, as my father was his teacher. He remained in the village during his early childhood years, with his mother, Elizabeth, who later returned to the village of his birth. On occasion he would visit, seeking out the teachings of my father and many others.

We rested by the riverbed and received his blessings upon us. We spoke quietly for many hours, sharing the many teachings we had received. John was a passionate man. I would liken him to my brother Lazarus, with his zest for life and his strong and compassionate nature. He knew of my ways and was accepting of them. When I spoke to John, I knew that he heard my voice, and received my teachings as an equal. I found this to be rare amongst the community of my brethren, and it heartened me.

Yeshua spoke briefly to John, after I had shared with him some of the teachings that I had received on the Isle of Crete. I saw John take note of Yeshua's countenance, and of the Light that encompassed him, I knew that John saw Yeshua's truth, and I saw a renewed vigor enter John as the dawning of realization came. He knew that the days that we had awaited were now present to us. I saw in my interior eye a transference of energy take place during this time. A new light entered into the physical form of Yeshua, and so too, did a light enter John. Each was raised to new heights before my eyes. The Light of Heaven had entered them, allowing each to be raised up, so that they could walk the path before them in truth, so that the blessings bestowed upon them may be awakened in full. I held this truth to my heart. I share it with you now so that all may know of the greatness of each of them, so that their path may be as a beacon of hope to all. Much changeover occurred that day, and I was witness to this truth, the Light of Hope was awakened.

There were many who gathered that day to be baptized in the River Jordan. They were renewed in spirit and in mind by the descent of the dove upon them, and received the teachings of The Baptist One. Yeshua as well reached out his hands upon them and invited in the Spirit of the Most High, and I, in my turn, placed my hand upon their forehead so that they may receive the Light of the Living Breath within them. The forgiving nature of each who came brought them to new heights within their cell structure. They were redeemed and brought forth into the Land of the Living.

The healing powers were strong in the hands of Yeshua, as he sought to lift the powers of self-destruction. John, in his turn, spoke in loving terms of the life to come for each who would seek it. He spoke of the days to come, and of the unifying force of love that would enter in full. He spoke of the period of preparation that was required for each who would seek us, that they may know this unifying force in full and receive it well into their being.

I stood by the shores of the River Jordan, and I heard the drumbeat of the Earth Mother, as she too prepared for the entrance of the Light that was to come. The earth quaked beneath my feet at times, as the unsettled nature of the earth's rhythms caused the earth's crust to quiver to and fro, as it was prepared for the descent of the dove upon it.

There are many who would hear my words and question my authority on these matters, I would say to them now…

The authority of the words that I speak comes not from the lips of my Being but from the Source of Light that dwells within me. Know that I speak these words of truth for all to hear, that they may know that the Land of the Living dwells within all who would seek it, and that Yeshua, who holds the Christ Light was a way -shower to this crown of glory.

May all rest in the peace of the Christ formation and speak in terms of love, so that a New Order may arise.

I rest now in this loving space and I speak of the Ways of Wisdom. May all seekers awaken in full to

*the Light of Redemption and know of the unseen glory
that resides within them. May it be brought forth for
the great glory of the Source of All.*

Many heard tales of the teachings that were
preached that day, and they came to join us in
the days and weeks to come.

We journeyed onward from this place at
the completion of our time with John. He
awoke to our departure, and we shared but
few words between us, as the path had been
laid bare to each of us in the night time hours
and we knew of what was to come. Our
departure was swift as we heard the
beckoning call of a New Earth and the
ministry of the Path of Light that was to
begin. We walked in silence, as we were
introspective to that moment in time. We
knew the Path would lead us to a time of
desperation and would require a resilience of
heart. I was heavy-hearted, though Yeshua
walked a straight path and remained strong in
his heart. He chastened me, reminding me of
my forecasted truth. He told me that I must

stand tall and strong in the face of all that was to come. I would often hear whispers in my head that caused me to retreat, to delay the path and to move into a state of unknowing. It was at these times that Yeshua would speak to me, scolding me gently, holding my hand tightly, and reminding me of my true heart and of all that awaited us. He was of a steadfast nature and remained within this true heart always.

We wandered aimlessly for a period of time until we received guidance to return to the Land of Galilee where we would find rest. There were many who knew Yeshua's name in this place. James of the Lesser remained by his side throughout our wandering, as did the Iscariot One and Matthew, the tax collector who was drawn to Yeshua's side by the simplicity of his teachings. There were women as well; his own mother, and Salome, also a mother figure to him.

Yeshua gathered many who were of a pure heart and of an intellectual capacity that allowed the teachings to enter them. There were others who were of a more masculine nature, they sought to purify the external form by way of the teachings but had little capacity to move more deeply within. It was in them that seeds of light were planted, to allow the growth from within and in time, to awaken the heart to truth.

In those days I spoke often, though however briefly, to those that gathered about Yeshua. There were many who would not hear my words. They sought to diminish me, to work against me, as my true form was not yet evident to them. Yeshua spoke in harsh terms to these ones and tried to re-establish a relationship of loving forbearance between us. My brother offered me help and kindness as well. There were many rumors that swirled about me. Many had little understanding of my days in Egypt and the teachings of Isis. They maligned the Ways of the Goddess and guarded their hearts against it. I spoke in wise terms and journeyed to the heart of many others, and it was to these ones that I sought to establish memory centers. It was often the women who gathered about me and listened to my teachings.

IX

Child of Light

I spoke often to one woman, who listened solemnly and spoke not a word. I welcomed her to my bosom and shared with her my Words of Light. I spoke to her of the kingdom within, the spiraling nature of her being, and the gentle flow of life that dwelled within her. We worked together for many months. I passed to her many initiatic rites that awakened the third eye opening and brought to her new knowledge of her truth. She began again, and walked with solemn countenance, as this was her nature. She walked with a spine that was straight and tall, and the words that she spoke were words of truth. She had a healing touch

and began to aid us in the Ministry of Light. I
came to know her well, she was known by the
name of Veronica, and gained residency in
our circle. She became as a councilwoman to
our band of travelers and walked firmly on the
Path of Light. She joined us from foreign
lands, a visitor, drawn to the Egyptian
teachings and the ways of the ancient
Priestesses of Isis. I knew her from this place,
though she was but a child when I departed
from the Egyptian temples. She became a
disciple to my teachings and listened to the
teachings of Yeshua, who mentored her as
well. He spoke in loving guidance and offered
to her the inner teachings of Melchizedek; she
became an Initiate in these ways. I speak now
of this one, as she has shown exemplary
service to me and the Ways of Light. The
memory center awakens within her now, as I
have implanted within her cell structure a
keepsake of my being that stirs the pot of
cellular remembrance, that she may be
awakened and speak my words of truth to all
who would seek the teachings of the Path of
the Way. I speak through her now, in this

moment in time, so that all may hear my words of wisdom.

I wish all to walk in the ways of truth, with a strong heart, and without fear of retribution from the masses. This time period from which you hear my words holds within it the key to the awakening of the heart. It is a time period that has been long awaited. Within each of you who hear my word dwells this truth and the key to remembrance.

Awaken now Little Ones. Be fearless in your ways. Remember.

✣

It was in the Land of Israel that we journeyed, the land of our forefathers and all who sought the Ways of the Torah. The Testaments of Old had forecasted these times of which I speak. They knew of the forecasted rising once again of the Son of Man in a death-defying leap. This would allow the resurrected form to return once again to the time space continuum, that the formless Christ may be awakened for all that would seek it.

There are few who know and understand these truths, that man is of a divine lineage. It was through the falling of mankind from his true form that he has become adrift, apart from this divine form. The Masters of Light have entered the time space continuum throughout the ages to bring light to this truth, that through the return to the Source Light within, all may be renewed and the Body of Light may be returned once again, in the resurrection of form. This resurrected form is of a spiraling nature and returns all who seek to their true source within. The star seed child within you is of a masterful form and is your truth. The Master Yeshua returned in remembrance of this light body and the star seed within each, so that we may return to the Child of Light and the true source of all knowing.

I too return you now to this Source of Light

through the teachings of my Being, by the translations that I place now before you. These translations that are before you, enter into your cell structures and draw forth the changes that are required for each of you. The language of light has been imprinted within each of you, and in truth, it is the language of Source Light, and so, through these translations of the light language, all truths known and unknown to man may be awakened. I speak of the Language of Light encrypted in the hands of light of Veronica, who transcribes my teachings. Hear now my words upon your Being, and receive well these Codes of Light, the Codes of the Christ Light Formation enter you now. They are codes that will draw forth-great change within you, allowing you to step forward as a Child of the Divine, the Inner Child awakens.

My journey with Yeshua continued for many years. We walked together, though sometimes apart. We travelled to foreign nations. We gathered together many followers of the teachings of the Path of the Way. Many healings occurred, as did many initiatic rites. We established upon the Earth a network of light, a grid system that enabled mankind to rise from The Fall. The vast teachings extended to many who were of fertile soil, and they received the seeds that we planted. We looked to the stars to guide us, and we anchored into the Earth's majestic heart. There occurred upon the Earth a revival of the Temple of the Divine. We established within the masses a center core that was a diamond structure.

We wish to establish this structure now within each of you who hear my voice. It will fortify and strengthen you for the coming days.

As the light increases so must the darkness, that it may be lifted. I wish to hold the hand of each of you during these times. I extend my hand to you now. Hear my voice and know that I speak to you. You are a Child of the Light. You must shake the dust from your feet. You must cleanse and purify. Prepare yourself to receive my healing touch and the voice of loving wisdom. You are embodied Spirits, full of the grace of the Mother image. Gaze now into the reflection pool of the watery depths of your being. Allow the inner reflections of this gaze to be of a loving nature. Receive my teachings of self-love and compassion, so that you may rise from these depths. Allow matters of self-inquisition to help you to find the voice in the darkness, the voice of the child within you.

She rises from these depths and states clearly and emphatically, "I am a Child of God. I know my truth and I speak now my name to the High Heavens!"

Rise, my Dear Ones, Rise.

I speak to you now from this place of the Highest Heaven, and you too may journey to this place. There is about you a hierarchical order that has imposed upon you a less-than

status. It entangles your heart and has placed
you in a deep sleep. Rise now from your
slumber. Awaken to your Truth. Know that
you are the strong and powerful sons and
daughters of the Divine Mother of All. She
dwells within you and speaks now to your
heart. Sever ties to all who would hold you
bound in a place of forgetfulness. Rise now.
We begin again.

Harden not your hearts to those who do
not know you or see you as they are in a place
of slumber. Their memory center has not yet
awakened to their Truth.

I say to you, "Begin again," in this moment
in time, and walk with strength, as you now
are the Leaders of Mankind. Rise to it.

The Law of One has entered in, and the
ganglions in the brainstem area - so long
neglected and forgotten, stir. The embedded
structures embroiled within it shall be
released, and all will come to know their
Name of Truth.

Rise, you are awakened Sons and
Daughters of the Light. Know of your
resurrected form. Begin now with me and we

shall rejoice in the living.

All who are disheartened shall come to know that everlasting peace dwells within them. All Seekers of the Light shall rise to new heights within their cell structures. I stretch out my hands to you, Children of the Light. You are embraced and received into the Womb of Creation. I rejoice in you.

The Master Yeshua is an incarnation of the Christ formation, which seeks to redeem the masses through the process of re-birth and the resurrection of form. We are twin flames and together we have walked to aid the masses, to redeem the world and to awaken the Heart of the Earth. We now awaken the True Form of Light within each of you who incarnates upon this Earthly form.

Harden not your hearts to these teachings Little Ones, as Christ is your Redeemer, so too am I the Chalice of Divine form. The partnership between the two awakens the masses to their own true nature. The ventricles of the brain are strong within each of you that you may know that these words I speak are words of truth. Turn not your ears aside and block the vibratory processes that seek to enter you now. Remember me, as I too carry within me the incarnation of the Christ form. I present it now to each of you; that the Light of Redemption may enter you.

You have fallen Little Ones, fallen into a deep slumber. I wake you now, and as the Christ has entered you, so too does the Chalice of Divine Function. The Cup of Abundance enters you, that you may enter the Land of the Living once again. Your true voice, the voice of the Living One, shall be shouted from the mountaintops and revealed to all. I pull aside the mask, Little Ones. I speak now your true name, that you may be vessels of pure light once again.

Fear not my teachings. Know that I embrace you, so that you may stand true and strong. In time the veil of separation that has parted us will be lifted.

I am The Magdalene One, the seed planter. I redeem the nations as I give birth to new life within each who would hear my name. The Master Yeshua stands by my side, together we walk. We begin again to aid the masses, to bring truth to all who seek it. You stand upon Holy Ground Little Ones, receive my breath upon you, and the Light of the Redeemer within you.

I journey now to your heart, and the heart within you shall know this truth and receive me.

The burning flames of redemption enter in, and the fires that burn reveal the true heart, Awaken!

You know now of my truth, of my physical journey upon the earthly plain. Close not your heart to me, as I am in truth, a woman born into a physical form, who has travelled vast distances to know the ways of the world and to dwell among you.

I have received you each into my heart; I wish to guide you to walk lightly upon this Path of Light, to enter into the quiet, and to seek the Ways of the Heart. In this way, all shall come to know their true name, and a Child of the Light shall walk once again in the form of the Angels.

�֎

I would aid you further, at a later time, in understanding of my travels with Yeshua and the later years of my life. At present, it is unnecessary. Rest well with this story Little Ones. Allow it to enter you. The Chalice of Divine Function shall awaken within you, and the burdens that hold you spellbound will be lifted from your heart. Hear me well. You are each here in an incarnated state to awaken, to walk a path of truth, to unburden the heart and to be fully redeemed. I guide you to a new end that these earthly dimensions may dwell once again in light.

I speak now to each of you in the silence of your hearts…I enter in as an indigo blue light, as I am the Way of Wisdom…

A gentle activation process has entered

each of you, as this is the time of the Great Awakening, and you have drawn to your breastbone these truths.

I embrace you.

I return you now to your daily lives. Remember my words. Allow them to swirl about you, entering into the silence of the heart, where all truths are revealed.

You are dearly loved.

I am the Blue Rose. I am the Path of the Way. Open your hearts and awaken.

~ *The Magdalene*

Afterward

You have received the story that I was asked to translate and share. You may have found yourself becoming drowsy or falling asleep as you read the story, this was the activation process entering you and awakening dormant cell structures.

As I was preparing to publish this story I was contacted by many people who had begun to receive messages from Mary Magdalene, or the light of the Blue Rose and found me through my website, they knew that I had information to share. She is calling to each of you, the time is now. Trust in your inner guidance, listen to your hearts, we are all being called to the roles we have been assigned from the Divine.

I have said in my introduction to The Magdalene's story that while Mary Magdalene answers many questions in this story, her story also stirs many more questions about The Magdalene's life. I have had to let go of any need for this story to be validated through the many other books written of Mary Magdalene's life. Each of these books, though the information within them may differ, contain levels of truth. This story and the symbolism contained within it serves the light and this time of awakening. I release it now to each of you for the Higher Good of All.

The Magdalene woke me this morning and said to me, "It's time to complete the writing. Take my hand, we will walk together and begin the new work."

We are all invited to take her hand and walk together; to receive the light of the Divine Feminine, to allow our hearts to awaken. The Magdalene has come to empower us, to help us to come to know and embody our truth and value on this earth. She has said to me:

"The rose, symbolic of the true nature within you. It's gentle unfurling is necessary that the strong scent of your being may be released. In full bloom, the rose basks in the rays of the sun and knows of its beauty."

It is important that we take time to quietly reflect on the words The Magdalene has shared with us, and to do this within our hearts.

When I began writing with Mary Magdalene, the words of her story streamed through me at a pace that was unnerving at times. I was often uncertain of the names and facts that she stated throughout the story. I had to be vigilant about my desire to research during this process, because it brought me into my thinking mind and out of my heart. My need for information would interrupt the process of allowing that was required for the natural flow of her words. At these times I was able to move back into my heart, to a space that allowed me to be unattached, and simply a vehicle for the story to be told.

It was only when the work was complete that I began to fully research parts of the story. I have included a Glossary of Terms at the end of this book for the many references made by The Magdalene that I did not understand or that I felt were not common knowledge to all of us.

As I continued the research, in certain instances, such as "the bark of a lemon to aid in aching joint", or, "the salted bread my mother made daily", I was unable to find any information to show that these statements were factual. When I reached a point that my need for evidence and facts turned into an anxious worrying, The Magdalene said to me very firmly "Enough! The story is sufficient to my purposes, it is complete." She made a quick gesture with her hand as if to toss away the worry. The Magdalene can be very strong in this way; she is patient and loving but has no tolerance for overthinking.

Many of you may wonder about the story of the woman Veronica, just as I did as the story unfolded through my hands. When this portion of the story was complete, Mary Magdalene said to me simply "This is you." Memories of this lifetime have stirred within me and continue to this day.

Since the completion of the writing of this story, The Magdalene has asked me to share her teachings and messages on the Divine Feminine and the Path of the Blue Rose.

Each of you who have received this story is in a process of awakening. Take time to rest, and to nurture and love yourself. Remember, this process is a gentle unfolding, it requires no effort, simply a remembering and allowing of your truth.

The Magdalene has told me that she has called to each of you so who has found this story; my prayer today is that this book continues to find its way into the hands and hearts of everyone who has been waiting to come to know The Magdalene, The Blue Rose, and that we all awaken to the Child of Light within us.

Glossary

1. Acropolis- an ancient citadel located on an extremely rocky outcrop above the city of Athens.

2. Annunciate-(pronounced a-nun-see-it) This word is not found as a noun except in the form "Annunciation", in Roman Catholicism when Gabriel appeared to Mary to announce that she would bear the infant Jesus. Mary Magdalene shares with me that it is a term used to portray that she was an embodiment of the light of the Living Word.

3. Aphrodite-An ancient Greek Goddess symbolized by the dove, rose and the swan. Also known as Venus, she represents the Goddess aspects of passion, creativity and dance.

4. Apostolate-This is used today as a Christian term which refers to a group

THE MAGDALENE

that is in service, the work of an apostle
or follower of a religion. Mary
Magdalene asked that I use this term.

5. Athena- A Greek Goddess known as a
warrior goddess as well as the goddess
of wisdom, weavery and smith craft.
She is also known as Minerva.

6. Artemis-A Greek Goddess also known
as the Roman Goddess Diana
(although some say she pre-dates the
Greco-Roman time period) she is the
huntress and the archer, protector of
the girl child and connected to the
forest and nature.

7. Atlantis- Atlantis is described in Plato's
The Republic, and later mentioned by
Edgar Cayce in his readings. It is
described as a utopian society with an
advanced technology that was
destroyed by a flood in 10,000 BCE.

8. Brighid- An ancient Celtic Goddess
known as the triple Goddess,

symbolized by fire, she is the patron of Healers, Poets, Childbirth, Smiths, and inspiration.

9. Super Conscious Mind- transcending human consciousness

10. Indigo Light- This is a dark bluish-purple light connected to the 6th chakra or third eye. This chakra is found between the eyebrows and is connected to intuition, higher states of consciousness and wisdom.

11. Elohim- In the Old Testament Elohim is a term used for God, but is also interpreted as a term for spiritual entities that work under God. In the Kabbalah, the Elohim are ranked in the Angelic Realm.
    The Magdalene shares with me that the Elohim are Creator Gods that aid in the process of manifestation.

12. Enoch- Great Grandfather of Noah, He is said to have written The Book of

Enoch in 2 B.C. and that he walked in faith and lived in an unknown land.

13. Frankincense-An oil used since ancient times and brought as a gift from the Magi at the birth of Jesus. It comes from a tree found in ancient Ethiopia. It can help in expansion of consciousness, protection, and meditation.

14. Grid Lines/Heart Lines- The ancients believed, as do modern day researchers, that there are currents of energy that form a network of energy lines around the earth. The earth is a living and breathing entity with both masculine and feminine energies which, when they intersect, form vortexes or energy points, similar to the physical body's meridians and chakras.

15. Isis-An Egyptian Goddess whose worship pre-dates 2350 B.C. through 6th century A.D. She symbolizes motherhood, fertility and magic. She was known as the Lady with 10,000

faces and Queen of Heaven in the ancient Mediterranean and Near East.

16. Land of Nod- In the Book of Genesis Cain was exiled to the Land of Nod. It is said to be East of Eden.

17. Light Body- This is the aura or the body of light that surrounds and pervades the physical form.

18. Melchizedek-He is mentioned in Genesis and The Book of Psalms as a priest and also as the King of Salem. He was a contemporary of Abraham, and was known as The Righteousness One. In The New Testament it is said " Jesus is a priest forever in the Order of Melchizedek".

19. Myrrh- This oil is one of the gifts brought by the Magi, it comes from a thorny tree and was used to anoint and purify. It is known for its ability to move the blood and its rejuvenation qualities.

20. Oil of Spikenard- A oil used by the ancients for blessing and protection, it was also known to aid in the regeneration of cells, healing of wounds and circulation of blood and lymph.

21. Star Seeds- Beings whose origins are from distant star or solar systems.

22. Temple of Luxor- A large Ancient Egyptian temple complex located on the east bank of the Nile River in the city today known as Luxor (ancient Thebes), it was constructed in approximately 1400 BC.

23. The Book of Life-According to Jewish traditions, this is a book in which God records the names of all of The Righteous destined for heaven.

24. The Temple Mount- Within the Jewish traditions, this term would refer to a hill located in the Old City of Jerusalem, the place where King Solomon built the First Temple. It is the holiest site in Judaism.

However, Mary Magdalene tells me that when she refers to the Temple Mount she is speaking of Mount Carmel. This is a mountain in northern Israel and has been considered a sacred place since at least the 15th century BC. Pythagoras visited this mountain. It is described as the most holy of all mountains, an altar was placed there by Elijah of the Old Testament. It has been closely associated with the Essenes, a Jewish mystical sect.

25. Qumran- Mary Magdalene says that this site was an ancient mystical site that was present to aid in the expansion of the bloodline of The Brotherhood of Light. It is located near the caves where The Dead Sea Scrolls were found and is believed by some to be a settlement for a group named The Essenes, a monastic group who lived in Palestine from 2 BCE – 1 AD.

26. Yeshua- This is the Hebrew or Aramaic form of Jesus.

ABOUT THE AUTHOR

Mary has been married since 1994 and has 4 children. She received a BS in 1988 and MA in 1989 as a Speech/Language Pathologist. She is a Spiritualist, Healer, Grid Worker, Spiritual Teacher, and an initiate and student of the Ancient Mystery Schools.

Mary has been a healer since 1999, a conduit for the Angelic Realm and Ascended Masters since 2005, and a channel for Mary Magdalene since 2013. Mary left her practice as a Speech/Language Pathologist in 2006 to dedicate herself more fully to service to The Divine. She uses the forums of small group classes, guided meditations, channeled writing, retreats and private energy sessions to share the teachings of The Divine Feminine and to aid others as well as the Earth in the process of healing and awakening.

To find out more about Mary and her work with The Magdalene, you can visit her website at www.bluerosehealing.com

Made in the USA
San Bernardino, CA
16 October 2018